PROVOCATIVE SUGGESTIONS

A No Bullshit Combination of Hypnosis, NLP and Psychology with Difficult Clients

Jørgen Rasmussen

www.provocativehypnosis.com

Also by Jørgen Rasmussen

Provocative Hypnosis

For information about this book or how to obtain
special discounts for bulk purchases, please contact:

Jørgen Rasmussen

Email: joergen@provocativehypnosis.com

Web: www.provocativehypnosis.com

Cover Design by Cybill Conklin

I would like to dedicate this book to my daughter Rikke

And a big thanks to my wife Marit, my mother Anne-Lise, my father John Åge, and Christian, Brian Mahoney, Lewis Walker, Bridget Mckenna, John Grinder and Jaye Manus for helping contribute to my book and make this possible.

FOREWORD

As a general medical practitioner I have spent the last 25 years using hypnosis, NLP and other therapeutic based technologies to effect change in my patients. I still remember the excitement of my early NLP days; the books, seminars and discussion groups and the first steps in using the various techniques. Much of it seemed like magic!

But...

I soon started encountering patients who didn't seem to fit with the seemingly effortless easy success of the seminar demonstration subjects. Over time and with varied conversations with others I began to see that the dreaded "left brainers" with poor visualisation and hypnotic capacity required more of a top-down cognitive and linguistic type approach (Beck's CBT and Ellis' REBT). And, incorporating those skills, for a time all was well in my world...

Then...

I started to encounter a different type of phenomenon. This was a person who despite using the best of my skills still remained stuck at the very edge of their map, whilst an almost identical presentation in another client went smoothly. Very puzzling indeed. What on Earth was happening here? I began to get the first hints of how there were various levels of conscious and psychological development and the difference between translational and transformational change. The former being change that didn't require a developmental leap, the latter requiring a much bigger shift in perspective taking and meaning making with significant impact across all contexts; New Skills versus a New Way of Being.

So...

I explored the writings of Ken Wilber and his Integral Model which incorporated much on developmental theory across many levels and lines from the likes of Suzanne Cooke-Greuter, Robert Kegan, Clare Graves and many others. These theorists all had one thing in common; great theories but little in the way of easy identification of presenting issues and practical utilisation at the coal face of everyday problems. Of these models, Kegan's ideas on mental complexity (especially the levels of socialised, self authoring and self transforming mind) was perhaps the most useful and I spent many hours trying to formulate his writings into a cogent therapeutic application.

Enter Jørgen Rasmussen...

Over the years I have known him, Jørgen has grappled with the very same issues—with One Big Exception. He is the only person I know working in the field who, through reading, training and much exploration, has managed to distil developmental theory into a coherent practical approach that deals with the real world—a complex and messy place where patients and clients don't come with attached labels, and where similar presentations and problems may belie very different levels of development. Jørgen has found telltale signals and signs that alert you to which type of issue you are dealing with—skills based or transformational. He knows how to sort through the mess, differentiate what is important from what's not, and knows just where to tap. And the key thing is—He Gets Results. And not only that, he can show you how to do the very same.

Caveat Emptor...(Buyer Beware!)

If you have read his previous book, *Provocative Hypnosis*, you will know that at times Jørgen takes no prisoners and can be 'politically incorrect'. This book continues at times in similar vein. If you are of a very sensitive nature and disposition then perhaps best not to read on! However if you are keen to find out just what you can do when the rubber really hits the road and you are dealing with the confusing complexities of human hurt in all its manifestations, trying to find a way through that engenders lasting change whilst being up to your eyeballs trying to sort out what's useful from what's not, then this is The Book for You. You will find many working examples both of translation of problems at the same level and find out just when this signifies a need for transformation to the next. At times it's messy stuff. And that will reflect your everyday experience with clients. You will go away much the richer for your read.

And as a bonus...

You may find out much more about your own current developmental level as you are led to the edge of your envelope in transforming to the next. Whilst undoubtedly gaining many new skills, you may well find a new Way of Being. And, more subtly, it will perhaps become clearer that you can only deal with clients who are at your current level of complexity or below. Maybe not politically correct, but with a great deal of Truth all the same.

Enjoy!

Dr. Lewis Walker, FRCP
General Medical Practitioner
Ardach Health Centre
Scotland
UK

CONTENTS

PRAISE

When I first read Jørgen's first book *Provocative Hypnosis* I was totally inspired to learn more about his work but I needed an answer to a burning question. Were these client stories really true?

From 2009 I started hosting 'Provocative Hypnosis' seminars and my questions were more than answered. Firstly because as I took Jørgen to the port one day I met his mother and her friend who, on dropping him off, told me all about the 'Anorexic' woman (her niece) who was now totally cured and had completely turned her life around...

It was signed and sealed confirmation for me and more importantly gives me the opportunity to second it all by saying to you, the reader, that I became witness firsthand to some of his client work since then and written about in his new book (*Provocative Suggestions*).

This is without doubt one of the best books I have ever read that totally surpasses his previous book by its sheer authenticity in writing and this man's humility when it comes to sharing his work.

I am privy to transformations in people that quite literally helped me to aim high when it comes to personal transformation and not become just another NLPer, Hypnotist, etc. Jørgen moulds his work from a variety of sources (that he not only acknowledges and gives credit where credit is due) but also layers the tools, tips, techniques, and more importantly the pitfalls of falling into certain ways of thinking/being when doing change work...

From start to finish he takes you inside the mind of the client and the mind of Jørgen Rasmussen and guides you, the reader, to become masterful in your client work.

This is in my opinion a writing masterpiece that will have you seriously improving and humorously laughing your socks off in both shock and awe...

Wayne Marsh, NLP Trainer and Serial Entrepreneur

•   •   •

When I was learning Taijiquan many years ago, I was always being told that I should choose a master and study deeply with him and him alone (or her)... That this was the only proper path to mastery. I ignored this and studied deeply with many (at one time studying concurrently with five different instructors). My mindset was that whatever skills I developed, they were going to be mine—embodied in MY body and, as such, personalised and unique. I was building MY art and MY skill, not just trying to take on board someone else's conception of what was 'right'. This approach paid dividends for me and I found myself rapidly accelerating past my classmates in terms of skill and ability.

Many years later, when I got into hypnosis/NLP/general brain-wrangling I took the same approach—study broadly and study deeply...explore and experiment. Generate an approach that made sense and worked for me (and I'm still doing it).

One person I have learned a phenomenal amount from—and count myself very fortunate to know—is Jørgen Rasmussen. Like me (only most likely bolder and braver), Jørgen is an explorer, tester and integrator...which seems to make him one of a rare breed.

Rather than going 'all in' with any particular philosophy

or school of Changework, Jørgen pragmatically explores and draws from a range of sources. But ABSOLUTELY NOT in a random or mismatched way. What he achieves is a cohesive hybrid, rigorously tested and thought through, where each element contributes to a powerful and unique gestalt.

But what is also true of Jørgen is that he is not building a static masterpiece or a signature approach that he can trademark and sell. He is always refining, adding, subtracting, and holds absolutely no allegiance to one fixed path, even of his own creating.

As I mentioned, Jørgen has been a huge influence on me in the four years I have known him, and he has introduced me to several sources that have become integral to my own work—especially Robert Kegan's developmental psychology, the REBT philosophy of Albert Ellis, *The Work of Byron Katie*, and William Glasser's 'Choice Theory'. In this book Jørgen will introduce you to his own integration of this work. Some aspects he speaks of explicitly and in great length, others shine through in the thinking. The heady brew that is created is presented via case studies and personal explorations.

I believe that this book will greatly serve anyone who works with clients in the capacity of helping them change behaviours, responses and results. It is a call to practitioners to escape from inward-looking silos and raise their eyes and minds to see what else is out there that may contribute to their evolution and efficacy.

James Tripp, Hypnotist and Transformative Coach

• • •

This is a remarkably practical little book. Jørgen has a very readable voice. The examples are really useful and something to recommend for practical therapists with some NLP/ hypnosis background, especially. The book does a good job in mixing stories with principles, the narratives are interesting and attention grabbing, then the explanations flesh out the story. I also like the way Robert Kegan's model is explained. It makes his approach very useful and some of what the more enlightenment-oriented followers of Ken Wilber's version of integralism have turned into esoteric mumbo jumbo quite sensible and useful for the therapist.

Chris Cowan, Co-founder of Spiral Dynamics and NVC Consulting

•   •   •

This brilliant book is raw, honest and of real value. Illustrated with compelling dips into the author's case book and clear descriptions of his bread and butter techniques, it has the potential to transform you as a therapist or better still turn you into a self-transforming agent of change.

Anthony Jacquin, Hypnotist and Hypnosis Instructor

PROVOCATIVE SUGGESTIONS

A No Bullshit Combination of Hypnosis, NLP and Psychology with Difficult Clients

Jørgen Rasmussen

"FUCKING WHORE" FIGHTS BACK

One early evening a few years ago, a former client called. As soon as she spoke, a voice of fear and pain began describing an awful event that had happened a few days earlier.

Maria had had a drink or two, but was not even near being drunk, when she left a garden party.

She walked home in a good mood the fifteen minutes it took to reach the gate that led to the nice garden outside the apartment complex where she lived.

A split second after entering the garden she was met with a piercing predatory stare from a man who started cussing and swearing at her, calling her a fucking whore.

The man charged at her like a wild animal and hit her in the face a couple of times before wrestling her to the ground and mounting her. She froze while he started pulling her skirt off with the intent of raping her. While she just barely managed a scream, he made a lot of noise with his cussing and swearing, enough to catch the attention of at least one neighbor with the balls and willingness to intervene.

Quickly, before the scumbag had the chance to rape her, the neighbor came charging out the door. The would-be rapist took off and ran into the summer night while the neighbor took care of the young woman. She immediately went into the shower and spent what felt like hours there. A couple of days later she reported the incident to the police, who sadly did not show much either of care or professionalism.

Her physical injuries were limited to some bumps and

bruises with a fat lip and a black eye to boot. Other things bothered her a hell of a lot more—flashbacks, sleep problems, nightmares and wild mood swings alternating between fear, anger, sadness, shame and feeling numb.

While describing the event and her aftermath experiences I noticed several things. I saw full congruency between her emotional state and how she described having experienced it. When she talked about fear her voice tone became higher and her breathing changed, and when she spoke about sadness and shame her voice tone changed in a way congruent with her emotional state.

In my experience this is a good sign. It suggests a client who can easily and deliberately access her symptom states and suggests at least a decent capacity for absorption and hypnotizability. Something else which really caught my attention was how she several times marked out, and leaned on, the following sentence: "*I just froze.*"

Not only did she mark it out and lean on it, she did so several times.

This is a magnificent gift from the unconscious. A marked-out word, phrase or sentence with a simultaneous "Christmas tree" light-up/access of symptom state (however subtle) offers something to be utilized in helping the client, for those astute enough to pick up on it.

The last thing I picked up was her congruent state of shame those times she said she was ashamed with herself for not fighting back. She had a background in traditional martial arts and was feeling ashamed of not defending herself.

Since I helped this client before I did a provocative hypnosis seminar in the United Kingdom, I chose to start the seminar by giving the participants the information I have just written here.

Dear reader, I would like to invite you along to the seminar. Just imagine you are in the seminar room having just heard this story. I've got two questions for you, and I would like you to deeply ponder them and come up with your own answers before reading what I did. Imagine that she is your client.

1. What would you want to know?

2. What would you do to help?

Seriously now, put the book away, go for a walk, chop some wood, whatever. Then do some deep reflection and write down your answers. Yes, I know, thinking is hard work, but you will get more out of both the book and your client work this way.

After some encouragement, the seminar participants started offering solutions, and without exemption they were all proposals for techniques and formats. Hot candidates were the infamous V/K dissociation (NLP phobia cure), time-line therapy, re-imprinting and hypnotic age regression with gestalt chair work and forgiveness therapy.

I was puzzled and somewhat disappointed with the responses, but rationalized them away thinking that not everyone spoke up and that quite a few might not be that experienced. How could they just ignore question one? Did they really not have any questions at all about the client and her life condition? How could they so quickly offer technique solutions without finding out anything about the client and her life condition?

So I got curious and repeated the same story plus assignment at several other seminars. I even did it in Holland so I could test the idea that the Brits were extra superficial in their thinking. I went further and asked several individuals the exact same questions.

The only changes in responses were that some people offered other techniques and formats such as thought field therapy and EMDR (eye movement desensitiziation therapy). Sadly, the following pattern emerged.

1. Everyone thought that this was something to be resolved in the office exclusively.

2. All solutions were proposals for techniques and formats.

3. Nobody suggested utilizing the marked-out "I just froze" or the shame of not fighting back.

4. The suggested solutions were made without wanting to know anything about the client or her life condition.

5. No-one offered a plan b or troubleshooting.

Unfortunately, these are symptoms of "technique absolutism". Clearly, these folks did not have a systematic roadmap that they could use to navigate towards solutions.

Instead their answers seemed to suggest a belief that the magic lies exclusively in a combination of selecting the right technique or format coupled with the technical skill level and congruence of the practitioner.

OK, here is what I did and my reasons for doing so:

The gate and garden she described sounded borderline close to the back entrance leading to my house.

I gave her instructions to arrive at my office with a bag containing a track suit and running shoes. Once there she was instructed to change her clothing before we got into my car. Up until this point she had no clue as to what she had gotten herself into. We parked close to my house. Then I got her into a High Gear suit—a Plexiglas helmet and protective gear all over the body. Tony Blauer, the inventor of the gear, designed it so that getting hit is painful, but you don't actually get hurt.

She laughed a bit when I told her that we were going to

simulate the attempted rape.

A lot of people underestimate how "real" such a self-defense simulation can get. After all, it's just a simulation and therefore fake. However, as she was soon to discover, even though she knew intellectually that it was fake, she responded as if it were the real thing.

A good friend and former self-defense student of mine, Tormod, was waiting inside the gate with his best combo of predatory stare and verbal vulgarity. He had donned his own High Gear suit (minus the helmet). After the stare and "fucking whore" verbal assault, Tormod put his helmet on and unleashed his "inner rapist" right in my back yard.

As instructed, he made a hell of a lot of noise and proceeded to hit her, wrestle her to the ground and rip her legs apart.

Maria responded just the way I had predicted: she *just froze.* (Remember the marked-out sentence and her shame of not fighting back.)

This was "as real as real"—the fear, the hyperventilation, the chaos and her freezing.

While Tormod was on top of her cussing and swearing and Maria's physiology was practically frozen with her hands seemingly cataleptic on the front of his Plexiglas helmet-covered face, I physically grabbed her arms and made her fingers rake and claw his face. Tormod realistically feigned responses, and I used her legs to kick him. Then I more or less lifted her body back to her feet and had her run for dear life.

To her surprise, she reacted as if it was real and forgot all about it being a simulation. I don't remember if she almost puked after the first take or the second, but it was that real.

We redid the whole thing several times. Gradually she unfroze the experience and while she needed me to physically move her body the first few times, she gradually took over and made me redundant.

The last few times, despite being exhausted, she fought

5

back on her own with full force and intensity.

That one session was all it took for all her symptoms to disappear. When last heard from she was doing well and has sent me several clients since then.

While editing this book I had the chance to speak to Maria. She had referred a client to me and I called her to say thanks. She was still doing great five years later. However, she correctly pointed out that we had done a session in the office, where we worked on disassociating from the memory, before we did the simulated rape event. My recollection is that we did the second session as the first one didn't seem that useful, and that it was during the simulation that the change happened. She is of the opinion that the first session was the most useful one. My version is more exciting, but she may be correct and it would be a lack of integrity on my part if I didn't include her comments here.

Before I offer my roadmap and reasoning, let me offer you a fair warning. Be alert and skeptical when listening to people, even highly skilled and experienced pros like me, when we offer our explanations. A lot of people in the self-improvement industry are advised to stop listening to anyone, in any field, who isn't doing well. Good advice, and I would like to suggest that you be just as skeptical of after-the-fact explanations no matter how brilliant the expert.

First of all, the models and explanations and stories I offer of what I did and how I decided what to do are *not* how it actually went down. Remember that memory does not work like a video camera. Rather it's a reconstructive process where my current mood, expectation, motives, similar experiences and a bunch of cognitive biases work together to whip up a story. A story and a *map*, however compelling and useful it may be, will never equal the experience and the *territory*.

Unfortunately, like any other human, my beliefs are mostly the result of years of paying attention to information that confirmed what I already believed while ignoring the stuff that contradicts my beliefs and assumptions. It's called tunnel vision and confirmation bias. Like you I am often ignorant of my deeper motives and create fictional narratives to explain my decisions, emotions and history without realizing it. And then I buy into my own bullshit. Ugh.

Sorry, Mac, but it's human nature. Let me be clear and specific here. I am not talking about lying or deliberately misleading anyone.

Shankar Vadantar, author of *The Hidden Brain*, offers a marvelous personal example of how we unconsciously deceive ourselves (and others) due to cognitive biases built into the architecture of our brains.

While on vacation at the beach, Vadantar went for a swim. Noticing the ease and increased speed of his strokes he became proud and impressed with himself. He attributed it all to his own technique and endurance. It was only while struggling with fatigue while swimming upstream he had his big eureka moment. The undercurrent had created his increased speed. Technique and endurance had little, if anything, to do with it.

It is a brain bias. We unconsciously create narratives where we credit ourselves with successes and blame outer circumstances for our failures. This way we protect our pseudo self-esteem.

This bias contributes to our stories and explanations being way too neat and tidy. Using language, we impose boundaries, categories and a sense of stability and order that's absent in the actual world.

My stories are also way too tidy and ordered. As Nasim Taleb likes to point out, we downplay luck, randomness and non-events.

Another problem with explanations (yes, even when the explainer is successful) is that experts often have no frigging clue as to how they produce their results, so may be compelled to just make something up. This may be especially true with genius performers in any field. This is one reason why Neuro Linguistic Programming co-founder John Grinder has so strongly emphasized modeling in a know nothing state (suspending attempts to understand and not listening to explanations) during his modeling projects.

A final issue is that experts will tend to attribute their success to being hard-working, having more integrity, etc. It may of course have much to do with it (or not), but my point is that this reflects human nature; we have a tendency to be natural hypocrites. A great formula for being a champion hypocrite seems to be built into our brains. We judge ourselves by our intentions (I only wanted to help) while we judge others based on the perceived consequences of their actions (I feel hurt—therefore you meant to hurt me).

If we succeed, we take full credit. Other people's success may have more to do with luck and family connections. When we screw up we blame external conditions (traffic wouldn't move and the train was late), but others' screw-ups may have more to do with their rotten personalities (he has no respect for others' time and is a spoiled brat). No wonder that quite a few polls show that most people think they are smarter, funnier and better drivers than most. The majority, at least in some polls, select themselves to be the person they know who is most likely to go to heaven.

Is it any wonder there is so much suffering in our relationships? Of course, things aren't that black and white, but it seems to be more accurate than not.

Ok, now that you have been thoroughly warned, let's get into it.

Commitment

Maria was very motivated and also willing to do serious work. Her symptoms were intense and had started after the incident. A client who is motivated as well as committed is usually an ideal client who is very likely to change. The intervention I chose for Maria is not one I would have chosen for a client whose commitment level and symptoms were low. A committed client offers you a wider range of interventions to select from, especially the dramatic and somewhat outrageous ones. Paradoxically, the clients who are deeply committed (willing to do whatever it takes) are very often the ones who change very quickly, even when their symptoms are very severe.

Our Relationship

As I mentioned previously, Maria was a former client. I had helped her change some deeply rooted fear-based issues in a couple of sessions a few years earlier. The results were lasting. She also sent me a friend, whom I was also able to help. As a result of this I had a lot of credibility in her eyes, and we trusted one another. We also got along well and had great rapport. I would not have chosen that particular intervention with a new client in her first session. Never say never.

Expectations

Since she had had an experience of rapid change the last time we worked together, she believed that she could change quickly. I utilized her expectancy by pointing out that since she had changed quickly the last time, and since her symptoms had only appeared after the incident it probably meant that when we changed how she remembered the incident she could change and do so quickly. This was very plausible to her.

9

Symptom Onset

None of her symptoms were present before the incident. This also suggests that a dramatic corrective experience is likely to be sufficient to make the symptoms disappear.

Marked-Out Sentence

The fact that she leaned on the sentence "I just froze" and went into that state as she did so suggested to me that her unconscious requested help unfreezing her experience. An obvious solution is to activate her symptom state and then help her unfreeze the experience. We could have done it using hypnosis. However, her background and identity combined with her training in traditional martial arts combined with her shame in not fighting back suggested a self-defense simulation in real time.

My own background was also relevant. I worked professionally as a reality-based self-defense instructor for 16 years. Sometimes, skills and competencies from other areas of life can be utilized in change work. My martial arts and self-defense background has been useful on a few occasions and has profoundly influenced my thinking.

Absolutism

Clients' symptoms are almost always connected with irrational absolutistic demands that they make of themselves, others and the world. In Maria's case she was telling herself that she *absolutely* should have fought back. When the reality was that she didn't, the result was a roller coaster of strong negative emotions. Her shame also suggested that she was downing and damning herself as a person, instead of damning her own actions while unconditionally accepting herself. I did not directly challenge her irrational demand that she absolutely should have fought back, nor did I attempt to teach her unconditional self-acceptance.

Instead I designed an experience where she could have a felt, embodied experience of both unfreezing and fighting back.

Hypnotizability

I use hypnotizability as a diagnostic tool. My own experience as well as decades of scientific testing on hypnotizability has confirmed that hypnotic capacity is a remarkably stable trait.

It seems to consist of absorption, dissociation and suggestibility.

- Absorption: the ability to become absorbed into some suggested experience to the point where it's "as real as real".

Those who are good at absorption can often get so into a movie that they actually need a few seconds to reorient back to the reality of being in the theater. Whereas those who score low only partly get into it and are always more or less monitoring their environment.

While absorption is something almost all great hypnotic subjects are good at, not all those who are good at absorption are good hypnotic subjects. Furthermore, there is a small group of people referred to as "amnesia prone" who both with and without suggestion often are amnesic for much of their experience. They are not necessarily good at absorption.

- Dissociation: If you have seen someone unable to remember their own name as a result of suggestion you have seen what's often referred to as deliberate or controlled dissociation.

The same goes for those who act out post-hypnotic suggestions and remain amnesic for both the suggestion and the act of doing it. The highly hypnotizable will sometimes, as a result of suggestion, develop amnesia for the entire hypnotic

11

experience. For some it can even happen spontaneously.

- Suggestibility: When I talk about suggestibility I am not talking about conscious compliance, obedience or gullibility—I am talking about the ability/tendency to respond non-volitionally to suggestion. An example would be the clients who, after being asked, "When you *feel your allergy* coming on...how do you know you *feel it now*..." respond by actually exhibiting teary eyes and a stuffed nose.

Those who are highly hypnotizable are great at absorption, dissociation and suggestibility. Knowing how hypnotizable your clients are offers you the chance to tailor-make your interventions to their hypnotic capacity. I am convinced that quite a few failures in both hypnotic and non-hypnotic psychotherapy can be—at least in part—attributed to this.

Maria was a pretty solid hypnotic subject. While the intervention I chose for her was applicable for all ranges of hypnotic ability, her hypnotic capacity opens the door for getting much of the same effect utilizing a hypnotic intervention. The lower the capacity for hypnotic responsiveness, the more you will have to rely on cognitive analytic and behavioral approaches.

Had she had little or no hypnotic capacity, the intervention I chose would likely be the only way to get results that quickly.

Responsibility

In my practice I have found that most people excel at the victim role. They blame external events and other people for their own emotional state. The more they make sense of their experience this way, the more energy they will use to manipulate other people to change so they themselves can feel better. When regular bitching and complaining doesn't quite

12

work, they will often unconsciously produce symptoms.

I tend to look at symptoms as choices, though largely not conscious ones. The most important factors are how people make meaning out of experience. Looking at symptoms as a combination of meaning-making and social roles offers a lot of choices for you as an agent of change.

Maria had little of that going on. She was well aware that she largely created her own symptoms, which is a big plus.

You can learn a lot about how someone structures their experience by discovering what they are willing and able to take responsibility for. From a structural perspective, a person can only take responsibility for something if he or she knows it's possible to take responsibility for it.

Useful questions to ask are: What does this client take responsibility for? What does this client *not* take responsibility for? What does the client not take responsibility for and *knows* that he or she does not take responsibility for? Just as revealing, what does he or she not take responsibility for and *not* know he or she is not taking responsibility for it?

These types of questions can help you discover how the person is selfing.

By selfing, I am referring to how the client defines the psychological boundary that distinguishes what is self and what is other. Specifically, which psychological processes the client claims as his own (inside the self boundary) and which processes he or she identifies as belonging to others.

Now, don't worry if this selfing stuff sounds like awfully abstract psychobabble. We will return to it later with practical real-life applications.

While we are on the topic of psychological responsibility, go back and read your answers to the two questions I asked. Then ask yourself the four questions I just asked. Notice, in light of these questions, the answers given in my seminar experience.

Consider the huge epistemological difference between a job position that requires you to do your job as defined by company instructions. Show up on time, follow the rules and do your job as defined by your superiors. This is one way of conceptualizing what it means to be responsible.

Now. Imagine a very different job position. Here you discover that it's not enough to do the right things as described by others. A whole new game awaits you. Your job is now to define for yourself what the right thing is and be willing to deal with the consequences whether they were what you intended or not. Being able to move from the first way of conceptualizing responsibility to the second requires a shift in how you make meaning out of experience.

The responses given from my seminar participants seem to be more in alignment with the first job description than the second.

The answers reflect them having internalized some ideology/system of change work, and now they are viewing clients through the filter of that system. Acting as a professional equals acting in accordance with so-called professional standards defined by proper authority of said psychotheology. This way of understanding responsibility corresponds with what developmental psychologist Robert Kegan calls socialized mind.

If you want to be an exceptional agent of change, this type of meaning-making is not sufficient. It's not sufficient to internalize some school of thought and then seek to act in accordance with proper protocol.

You've got to evolve. You've got to be able to take a step back and reflect. Reflect on the assumptions, concepts, professional guidelines, etc., so that you can use or discard them based on what your inner seat of judgment and real-time feedback tell you.

Specifically, how can you design a "therapeutic" context

most conducive to change for your client? This requires what Robert Kegan refers to as a self-authoring mind. Personally I think it's a requirement for really consistent effective work as an agent of change. More on this topic later.

Back to how I decided on a model of how to work with Maria. Earlier I briefly mentioned life conditions. Let's see how they applied in this particular case.

Legal Matters

I was somewhat surprised that none of the people who responded to my question addressed this issue, especially in a serious assault and attempted rape. In Norway, where I live, hypnosis is illegal unless you are a government-licensed medical doctor, psychiatrist or psychologist. In many countries, if the courts discover that someone's memories have been "hypnotically enhanced" that person's testimony will be dismissed. That is something to consider in cases where someone's symptoms are connected to a criminal or civil matter which may end up in court.

Fortunately she did not consult with a psychiatrist or a psychologist in this case. If a client "gets worse" and commits suicide, it's likely that you as the perceived charlatan will be blamed. Since 2006 I have had a strict policy of only working with people who are not part of the psychiatric system—people who are not seeing a psychiatrist, are not on psychiatric drugs or on welfare for their symptoms.

Competing Commitments

Sometimes clients may have simultaneous competing commitments. On the one hand they may sincerely want to release their symptoms. Simultaneously, outside of conscious awareness, there may be other competing commitments that "have them" such as suffering as much as possible in court to ensure that the mugger or rapist be punished as harshly

15

as possible. Strong symptoms and a "ruined life" may also ensure better money compensation and lucrative welfare deals.

I prefer thinking of this as competing commitments rather than secondary gains. While secondary seems passive, the term competing commitments presupposes that people are unconsciously adjusting their behavior in alignment with their commitments. You had better be aware of these sorts of issues and plan accordingly as you set the terms for your relationship with clients and the interventions you select.

Maria's case was not being investigated, so the chance of it ever going to court seemed unlikely in the extreme.

She was also a well-educated woman, passionate about her work and without any plans for a compensation or welfare deal.

Cultural Surround

I never accept clients who are part of phobia groups or similar groups—I learned the hard way. More often than not, membership in these groups will be connected to the person basing his or her identity and social life around maintaining some issue that they simultaneously claim to want to solve. While they may sincerely want to solve their issues, be prepared for deeply rooted competing commitments connected to both belonging and their self-concept and identity. Highly hypnotizable clients as well as those primarily operating out of a socialized mind are at extra risk.

To be fair, support groups can be useful to some people. David Spiegel documented that women with terminal breast cancer who met every week for ninety minutes lived twice as long as members of control groups. They also had less pain due to both self-hypnosis techniques and social support. But a terminal cancer group consists of people looking to live better with their disease, not of people looking to overcome it.

Maria was not part of any support group and as far as I know no-one had anything invested (herself included) in her maintaining her symptoms.

Medication

Maria was not on any psychiatric drugs. People who have accepted a psychiatric disease framework and who use psychiatric drugs offer some challenges. One challenge is the victim role and the passivity it implies alongside the implication that the client suffers from a broken brain or chemical imbalance and can't really do that much to change.

Another huge issue is that the medications themselves often produce the exact symptoms that they are supposed to resolve. Had she been on, say, antidepressant medication her symptoms could have had more to do with the drugs than anything else. If you choose to do change work with people on psychiatric drugs you may, even if successful, obtain so-called ghost results—results associated with the drug states that don't continue once the person is off the drugs. In addition, you may need to deal with withdrawal symptoms, which many psychiatrists present as proof of how ill their patients are and how much they need the drugs.

I used to work with people who were on psychiatric drugs. For the reasons mentioned above and a host of others, I have not done so since 2006.

How Did the Change Happen?

Remember that it's not the incident itself that resulted in Maria's mood swings, flashbacks, fear and nightmares. The incident probably lasted less than a minute and was over as soon as it was over.

If someone is traumatized afterwards it's due to how they keep reconstructing the pictures, sounds, body sensations and story around the incident, and that is a dynamic process. By activating her symptom state and having her do a tailor-made reconstruction (with unfreezing and fighting back) the memory is reconstructed and stored in a brand new way.

SELF-DEFENSE TRAINING

On a few occasions I have tasked clients, especially those exposed to mugging and rape, with taking up realistic self-defense training. On some occasions I have personally organized the type of simulation that Maria went through.

I am simultaneously puzzled and disappointed that the psychotherapists, NLP folks and hypnotherapists who work with these issues don't seem to think alongside these lines at all. First of all, the type of simulation just described can be magnificent in helping people resolve trauma. Realistic self-defense training can also help people develop skills and insights that reduce the chances that they will be victimized in the future. I'm talking about skills and embodied insights into how to avoid violence, how to verbally defuse situations as well as fear management and fighting skills. Last, but not least, even if they never have to use their skills in the future, the insights and experiences can help them create a story for themselves regarding fear, violence and human nature that is both useful and reality based.

If you as an agent of change won't look into this topic then I highly recommend that you make a connection/working relationship with competent reality-based self-defense instructors in your area. There are a few essential points to understand so that you know whom to consult. The first myth we had better kill is the idea that martial arts training and self-defense training is the same thing. Most of the time, they have virtually nothing to do with each other. Sometimes there is a partial overlap at best. What's called martial arts and self-defense training can be broadly classified into three categories.

1. Traditional Martial Arts

Here you learn the rituals, philosophy and techniques of a traditional martial art. Aikido, Hapkido and Jujitsu would be well-known examples. Discipline, respect for tradition and technical purity are emphasized. People practice chore-ography under controlled conditions where everyone coop-erates, typically against someone "attacking" them with tra-ditional techniques. While studying a traditional martial art can have many benefits, it does nothing to prepare someone for a raging sociopath bent on taking your head (or your vir-ginity) in a real street encounter. Nothing that is, but equip-ping its participants with a false sense of confidence and a first aid kit that isn't functional. I think it's highly unethical not to differentiate between traditional arts training and re-alistic self-defense training.

2. Competitive Martial Arts

Welcome to the world of judo, kickboxing, wrestling and mixed martial arts. A boxer actually learns to take and give a shot. A judo player actually gets thrown to the mat and tapped out with an armbar. Choreography is eliminated, and the participants learn what works against a resisting opponent. The techniques are more realistic, and combative training helps the players to develop endurance, strength, mental toughness and resiliency as well as the ability to tri-umph even when fear and pain are present. While some of

19

these sports such as Muay Thai and mixed martial arts are hardcore (you don't want to mess with these guys), the obvious drawback is that the participant is training to win in a sport setting with rules, a referee and an opponent they have consented to fight. Furthermore, what a professional fighter can do is largely irrelevant to the novice who has neither the attributes nor the skills of the well-conditioned fighter.

3. Reality-Based Self-Defense

Ironically, while many polls have shown that people's main motive for taking up a martial art is self-defense, very few actually practice self-defense. Unfortunately the masses seem more into rituals, belts and uniforms than the real thing. The main difference between a competitive sports fight and a self-defense situation is *consent*.

There is a huge difference between preparing for and consenting to a sports fight with rules, regulations and a referee versus being suddenly mugged at knife point or sucker-punched. A realistic self-defense program has got to emphasize how you can avoid violence by understanding predator/prey interactions. It's got to emphasize verbal defusing tactics and how to read a setup for a sucker punch as well as how to use verbal distraction and non-violent postures to set up stun-and-run tactics.

Fear management skills are of utmost importance. Often the relative calm of the dojo or training room is so different from the fear, adrenalin rush, chaos and hyperventilation of a real encounter that the practitioner has no access to his skills—hence the need for practicing while in a similar state as the one will likely be in real time. That's why a full-speed simulation of attempted assaults using protective gear, role playing, dialogue and solid contact is essential. It's still fake, but it's as close to reality as you can get and a lot more realistic than sparring. The techniques should be based on what the body wants to do (flinch) without training.

I learned to do this kind of stuff from a brilliant strategist named Tony Blauer back in 1996. Other excellent sources in addition to Blauer, are Richard Dimitri in Montreal, Canada and the famous martial artist, author Geoff Thompson in the UK. Systems like Krav Maga also often offer excellent training.

WALKING THE BANANA

Susann was an engineer in her late twenties with a social anxiety problem, or so she said.

Our first conversation started like this:

Susann: I suffer from social anxiety

Jørgen: Not really. It's more accurate to say that you scare yourself with how you think about social situations, and since you are here, you are quite good at it.

I very often interrupt clients like this right away. I don't want to play within a mental illness frame where she is a victim and I am supposed to fix her. The frame I am introducing is one where anxiety is something she is *doing*. It's due to how she thinks of social situations, and it's a skill/achievement.

Another reason for interrupting is that clients, especially if they have seen a therapist or two, often go right on telling their story. An interruption jolts them out of that mode. And I want to know if the client resonates with the idea that they largely create their own symptom. Some people get it, and are looking for tools and techniques. Others get offended, irritated or confused. Their experience is that their own internal experience just happens to them and that it's caused by other people and circumstances/events. These folks usually look for a therapist or technique to fix them (hypnotize me and make it go away), or for someone to offer understanding and insight into why they are the way they are. They often believe that this insight will change them. Also, since they believe that others and external events cause their feelings and symptoms, they may look for ways to manipulate others into changing so that they can feel better. While there are other ways of making sense out of experience, most clients fall somewhere between the two positions. The experience of "people and events do it to me" corresponds with a way of selfing that is socialized, and the latter experience corresponds with a way of selfing that is self-authored.

Susann seemed like a mix.

She immediately agreed and said that the problem lay in her being negative and that she didn't have enough self-esteem. She further commented that she sometimes had good self-esteem when others were supportive and praised her intelligence.

The astute reader will notice that she isn't really talking about *self*-esteem. She is talking about *other*-esteem, implying that other people's approval was the source of her sense of self-worth. While on the one hand she talks about realizing that it's her own thinking that is the problem, she is clearly operating out of a socialized mind.

Jørgen: When do you feel the most anxious?

Susann: In situations where I risk looking stupid. I can't stand it when people think I'm stupid. Even if they don't think so, just the thought that they could think I'm stupid is what sets me off.

Jørgen: When do you think that and scare yourself the most?

Susann: When someone asks me my opinion in meetings, if I have to present something, or even in playing simple games with friends and especially colleagues. I can't handle it if people think I'm stupid or weird.

Notice her *absolutism*. She doesn't merely *want* to be thought of as intelligent, she thinks she *needs* it.

> **Jørgen:** OK, let's say you screw up and people around you think you are stupid. Imagine that now...what is it about that that scares you the most?

I prefer to push people to the edge of their map by asking them what's the worst that could happen...get them to imagine it...and then to ask them what it is about that that scares them the most.

> **Susann:** If people think I'm stupid I get scared and I'm shameful. My self-esteem crumbles.

> **Jørgen:** So...if you think that other people think you are stupid then your sense of self crumbles.

> **Susann:** That's it, especially if it's important people.

> **Jørgen:** Other peoples' evaluations, or at least what you think they are, make up your self-worth? If you think that they think you're stupid, that equals low self-worth, and if you think they think you're intelligent, then you're suddenly "good enough".

Notice how different this is from someone who evaluates his or her own self-worth depending upon whether he or she acts/performs up to his or her own internal standards.

Someone who has differentiated her *self* from the ideas she has internalized, who has a self that is the generator of values, standards and goals would not feel ashamed or anxious due to thinking that other people think she is stupid. A person whose sense of self is made up by her relationships is on shaky ground if she perceives that others don't approve of her. Hence the idea that she *needs* approval.

A person who is self-authoring could still feel anxious and shameful, but it would be due to not living up to internal standards. Perhaps she demands that she be an excellent speaker so that she can reach some goal, then rates her overall value as a person on how well she does.

A bit further into our conversation I acted as if I thought she was stupid and noticed that she did "go into state". I anchored her problem state visually and auditorily using a different voice tone, some embedded commands and a gesture. I noticed her self-anchor (where she touched herself) imitated it and said, "feel that."

Interestingly, none of the anchors worked to retrigger her state. In addition to this she had a really hard time deliberately triggering the problem state using her own imagination. Neither did she respond well to my attempt at hypnosis. While she could imagine the context and shift her own visual and auditory sub-modalities, doing so deliberately only minimally shifted her state.

One choice would be affect bridge hypnotic regression to reconstruct some old memory imprints around "stupidity". But her hypnotic capacity didn't seem up for it. Neither did anchoring and sub-modality formats have much use. I knew that our work would have to combine reasoning and disputing absolutistic thinking with behavioral methods.

I had two things that I wanted to do. One was to help her dispute the belief that she needed approval and replace it with merely strongly preferring it.

Along the same lines it was essential that she discover and have a felt experience of being able to handle it if she thought someone perceived her as stupid...to develop a self more distinct from the ideas she had internalized.

Maybe even more important, I wanted her to develop unconditional self-acceptance instead of self-rating based on either perceived approval or being able to live up to self-generated values. To me it seems obvious that as long as people irrationally rate themselves as human beings, by equating personal worth with either accomplishments or approval, they will continue to demand that they must succeed, that they need love and respect, and that their lives absolutely should be the way they want them to be.

In my opinion, the writing and work of Albert Ellis, founder of Rational Emotive Behavior Therapy (REBT), argues the merits of a non-absolutistic mindset as well as unconditional self- and other-acceptance better than anything else I have encountered. I highly recommend using the philosophy of REBT as a source and utilizing NLP and hypnosis in the service of that philosophy. I will argue this point through examples as you progress through this book. Unfortunately, in the world of change work, NLP and hypnosis formats are often used in the service of absolutistic philosophies and it often contributes to people ending up more neurotic as a result.

In the second half of our first session I did my best to persuade Susann to adopt a philosophy of unconditional self-acceptance—that she can rate her actions, decisions and thinking as good or bad, useful or not useful according to some set of standards in a specified context, but to skip the part about rating herself as good or bad as a human being. That her running speed could be good enough (or not) to qualify for the Olympics, but rating herself as good enough or not good enough is irrational and a source of anxiety and shame. That she can act kindly or cruelly but not be a kind or cruel person. That winning doesn't make her a winner and losing doesn't make her a loser—it just means that she won or lost in some context.

Of course, some people succeed a lot in one or several aspects of life. But to be a "successful person" presupposes that one succeeds in all contexts, all the time. Clearly, something no-one can live up to.

Albert Ellis argues that as a person you have done both kind and cruel behaviors, have won and lost, made great and stupid decisions, etc.—that it's impossible to rate one's total self. First we would have to have access to everything the person has ever done (clearly impossible). Assuming we could actually do that, we would have to have solid scientific criteria for evaluating and adding up the person's acts and intentions (good luck).

And, of course, tomorrow the whole thing will shift due to new decisions and actions; the self is too complex to rate, and the idea of rating human worth based on any standards seems very shaky. One can rate one's decisions and actions based upon real-life consequences, but it's important to be aware of hindsight bias in doing so. A decision may seem horrible when we look at the consequences of acting on it. In hindsight, it seems obvious that we should have "known it all along", but that doesn't necessarily mean the information was available at the time of decision. Even if something turns out badly, it may still have been the best decision based on what one knew, or could have known, at the time.

This hindsight bias affects us all. Once we shift our beliefs or have an insight, we have a tendency to unconsciously reconstruct history and memories so that it seems obvious that we knew it all along.

A common example illustrates this. Have you ever found an old diary from your teenage years, only to be horrified at how different you were from the story you have told others (and yourself) about how you actually were?

A final argument for adopting a philosophy of unconditional self-acceptance is that once we define ourselves as, say, an intelligent person, it's easy to be more concerned with maintaining that identity than with learning something new. Some studies show that kids who are labeled and praised for being intelligent do less well over time than those who are praised for what they do. The ones labeled as intelligent often become concerned with making mistakes and avoid people and activities that make them feel stupid.

It's quite anxiety-provoking for someone with an identity of intelligent or a kind person to be exposed to feedback that threatens that self-concept.

If one identifies as a compassionate person based upon performing compassionate acts, then behaving like a jerk must mean one is a jerk. Quite an incentive to sweep the feedback under the rug or create a story that the other person "deserved it".

Naturally, people who don't rate themselves still prefer succeeding and being praised, but since contrary feedback no longer threatens one's self-concept, it's not nearly so anxiety- or shame-provoking. Still, it's one thing to claim some of one's traits may be great, it's something else to claim that one's *essence* is.

Susann seemed to really like this philosophy; however it was still more or less an intellectual insight, not an embodied insight.

Session Two

It was time to hit the streets with a solid marathon session. Our tools were a local shopping mall and a notebook for a writing task. Since she had leaned on "I can't handle it when people think I'm stupid or look down on me", I wanted her to have experiences of being able to handle it and to practice unconditional self-acceptance. It was time to develop a self that had more distance from the ideas she had internalized.

Since she was motivated and committed, it was not difficult to get her to agree to my "devil's pact", specifically that she do whatever I asked provided it wasn't unethical, illegal or fattening. Women don't seem to care so much about illegal or unethical, but knowing that it won't be fattening brings relief followed by compliance. The deal was whatever I did, she was to imitate.

Susann was quite concerned as we approached the mall, but she had not anticipated what happened next. I walked up to a woman and initiated a seemingly normal social conversation. As soon as the woman relaxed and engaged in the conversation I got down on one knee and started sweet-talking her nonexistent dog. While the woman was confused, and before she had time to freak out, I stood back up and resumed the normal social situation.

People usually size you up quickly and put you into some category. Once you are either OK or weird, people know how to treat you. It's something else to first put yourself into one category, break it briefly, and then without hesitation resume the original role. The woman struggled with knowing how to respond; it was (at least to me) quite entertaining. However, after having a longer second chat with the dog that wasn't there, I entered promptly into the "weird" or "slightly psychotic" category, and my new friend took off...fast.

Poor Susann looked like she was about to completely freak out, but stayed true to her word and performed the same stunt shortly thereafter. After her new friend took off, I handed a red-faced Susann a pen and a notebook. I wanted her to inquire, while emotionally in the eye of the storm, whether it really was true that she couldn't handle it. And what did the other person's perception of her mean about *her*. Did she have to rate her overall self as "good enough" or "not enough"? And was it really true that she *needed* the other person's approval, or did she merely prefer it. These were the types of questions I had her use her reasoning skills to explore.

Our next stunt showcased her quite-convincing acting skills. I walked up to people at random and with a heartfelt smile acted as if they were old friends.

The day's most entertaining moment came when Susann walked up to a woman in her early forties who was accompanied by her two kids. "Christine! How have you been?" A look of confusion appeared on the woman's face. While I don't know if it's so, I suspect the woman's name might have been Christine. Susann went into a colorful story, seemingly without shame, about them having spoken at a mutual friend's dinner party some time ago. Susann conned her into it and for a little while all was fine. Then, without instructions from me, Susann knelt down and started sweet-talking Christine's nonexistent dog. Christine suddenly realized that Susann was bat-shit crazy, grabbed both of her kids hard and yelled "Run, kids!" The kids obviously didn't sense any danger and hesitated, which only resulted in the scared mother more or less dragging her reluctant kids away. Susann's face flushed in some combination of red and pink as Christine, from a distance, told her kids that they had to get away from that crazy woman who could be dangerous. Still, a little laugh emerged between the waves of color on her face.

STEAK AT A BAKERY

Susann's next assignment was to congruently demand getting a steak at a bakery. She had to spend at least ninety seconds coming up with the most idiotic arguments for being served a steak at the bakery to ensure that the baker and customers viewed her as ground zero dumb.

More and more Susann discovered that although she was way out of her comfort zone, she could in fact handle it. And she discovered for herself that she didn't absolutely need anyone's approval, even if she wanted it.

The day's grand finale was pretending that we were religious nutcases attempting to get people to accept Jesus Christ as their personal savior.

After entering a video game store she looked into the eyes of the guy behind the counter and said, "You look like you have sinned a lot. Are you ready for forgiveness? Will you accept Jesus Christ as your personal savior?"

The interaction between the two of them was hysterically fun to watch. He—visibly uncomfortable and trapped in the damn store—used every excuse he could muster for why he couldn't talk about a topic like that at work. She did an even better job at countering them. While he didn't want to accept Jesus Christ as his personal savior, Susann proved to herself time and time again that she could handle it.

Her next tasks were done a few days later with a friend. One of them was an old shame-attacking exercise I have borrowed from Albert Ellis. It consists of walking a banana on a leash in public like one would walk a dog. Somewhat surprisingly, her outgoing and normally courageous friend took off and left her walking the banana herself among the crowd of people at Aker Brygge in the heart of Oslo city.

Quite a few people stopped to compliment the banana. She documented it all and sent me the picture as proof that she could indeed handle it.

MAUREEN THE MUSTURBATOR

"I'm wondering: Who here has strong Nazi sympathies? Please raise your hand." I raised my own hand and watched looks of confusion, laughter and slight anger on the faces of the seminar participants during a seminar in Doncaster, United Kingdom.

If morning coffee doesn't do the trick in waking clients or seminar participants up, then congruently accusing them of being Nazis usually works wonders.

My next question got even stronger responses. "Who here is a religious nutcase?"

Maureen had a strong non-verbal response and abruptly sat up, stretched her arms out, and leaned back. I accuse a lot of my clients of being religious nutcases. The reasons for doing so will soon be clear.

At the first break Maureen came up to see me. Somewhat sheepishly she said that John Grinder had sent her. "Ok," I replied. Maureen smiled and said she had strong anxiety issues, couldn't sleep and was also irritable and angry. Could I help her?

When I asked her, "What's this...?" while mirroring back her nonverbal response to the religious nutcase question, she said that she used to be a religious fanatic for many years, but had left religion and was *absolutely not* religious any more.

She started talking about her severe anxiety issues. Working in the NHS (National Health Services) she was part of decision making on serious matters in the legal system: Should that rapist get parole? Will that robber commit new crimes or can we release him yet? I noticed that Maureen used "have to" and especially the word "must" every time she gave an example of her issue—We *must* make the right decision. I *have to* be professional at all times, and I *must* not make a mistake.

Maureen was clearly very motivated and "went into state" when she talked about her issues. Very responsive indeed.

I offered to use her as a demo subject up on stage if she promised to agree to my devil's pact: "I have a solution that is extremely likely to succeed. It's not illegal, dangerous, won't hurt anyone and it's not fattening. I need for you to accept to do whatever I tell you, and shake my hand, *before* I tell you what it is."

To give credit where credit is due, I have borrowed this line of thinking from Jay Haley and Milton Erickson. They both used this to build commitment, suspense and response potential and get clients engaged.

While they would often say that they had a solution that was guaranteed or almost guaranteed to work, I have skipped any mention of guarantee as I believe that it inspires exactly the absolutistic mindset that often drives their symptoms. Another slight modification is throwing in the promise that it's not fattening to get a little laugh and to allow them to feel some humor about it.

Maureen said yes to the devil's pact. Immediately after the break Maureen was in front of the other participants, and once again, she easily accessed her anxiety when talking about it as well as heavily emphasizing the absolutistic "have tos" and "musts" with the same dogmatism and intensity as she had during the break.

As soon as she stopped talking I looked at her intensely,

and once I could see that I had her full attention I said, "Maureen, you are in front of people.... Didn't you know it's a sin (tapping her puritanical tendencies) to *musturbate*...and to *musturbate* in public?"

Maureen's face flushed and she sternly said that she had done no such thing.

"Don't lie, that's another sin.

"I must succeed, I must not make a mistake I must make the right decision...everyone can hear that you are *musturbating* like crazy."

The participants had a belly laugh and Maureen's face flushed again, followed up by rolling her eyes and exclaiming "Oh, God!" before she also started laughing.

Jørgen: "Now, honestly, what's this bullshit about not being religious and having left religion behind.... You're still a religious nutcase. After all, how do religious nutcases conceptualize it? There is the one truth, taken from one source. Then you have black and white thinking with a hell of a lot of musturbation. Absolute commandments to be dogmatically followed by all people, at all times, in all contexts. If you do, you get to heaven for eternity while the infidels get to burn in hell. Oh, then you have the ethnocentric morality with in-group/out-group. If you have the right beliefs you have rights, otherwise you are destined for damnation.

"The only difference here, Maureen, is that you want to be god and the guidelines of the NHS have become Holy Scripture."

Those of you who have studied the work of Clare Graves, or Beck and Cowan's Spiral Dynamics model, will recognize the description of DQ or blue ^{V}MEME system at work.

All the musturbating was the base for Maureen's neurotic symptoms. While she claimed to have left religion behind, her thinking was absolutistic and dogmatic, and she had internalized a lot of religious nonsense and professional guidelines through which she was viewing the world.

These internalized norms and rules had *her*; she was viewing the world through them.

What I wanted to do was to help her *have* these notions and rules. In other words, the ability to look at those ideas so she could have more choice and determine for herself to what extent these rules and assumptions were useful in some context.

The intervention on stage helped bring her musturbation up as something that no longer had her, but something she could see clearly and begin to have more choice about. It was time for a real-life task designed to both turn her demands into preferences and also to at least begin to develop from a heavily-socialized meaning-making system to a more self-authored one.

I reminded Maureen of our devil's pact. Utilizing her puritanical tendencies and religious background, I gave her the following task: Every time she found herself acting this way she had to do a public confession and admit that she was musturbating.

The following Monday she once again started musturbating in a meeting. True to her word and handshake, she honored the devil's pact. A colleague asked her a question and she immediately seized the moment and told her colleagues, "I have to make a confession. The last few minutes I have been sitting here musturbating intensely."

The room got completely quiet. I imagine these types of confessions are not a common occurrence in the NHS meetings.

After a few seconds she told them: musturbating as in "we *must* make the right decision" and "we *must* not make a mistake".

Half the people burst out laughing and the rest were completely silent.

During the seminar she told me that she was struggling with insomnia and that she hadn't had a full night's sleep in a couple of years.

I tasked her with closing her eyes as soon as she lay down to sleep and to deliberately musturbate like crazy with vivid sexual imagery. The sexual imagery scared her so much that she escaped by falling asleep. She had her first full night's sleep in a couple of years.

Doing the confession task over time gradually loosened up her musturbatory tendencies. She replaced her compulsive "have tos" and "musts" with preferences—strong preferences—and felt the experience of having choice.

The results were dramatic and lasting. One year later Maureen told her story at a new seminar. Her compulsiveness and anxiety issues had virtually vanished. Her relationship with her daughter had changed from a bad one with much anger and irritation to a very warm and mutually supportive one. And she was sleeping well.

THE RELIGIOUS ATHEIST

"You sneaky bastard...." Those were the first words out of Tom's mouth when he called me a month after our last session together. Chuckling, he told me that he just couldn't do it anymore. The "it" referred to his strong habit of angering himself. Tom identified with being a very rational person who was also an atheist to the core. He had no time for silly nonsense like religion.

Early in our acquaintance, I had asked him if he was religious to see if I could set him up.

Once we started officially working with his angering habit I stopped, looked at him intensely until I had secured his full attention, then I said, "Tom...your problem is that you're a religious nutcase—a full-blown fanatic."

The words were spoken with utmost sincerity and full congruence. Tom was a bit taken back, but somewhat confused and bewildered since he could sense that I wasn't kidding. This was not, as a rational atheist, what he expected. The idea that he was a religious nut was preposterous. To show him what I meant I explained that angering means that someone has broken your rules. That if he is angry at himself then that means that he has failed to live up to his own demands or standards in some context. If he is angering around his wife (which he was) then his wife was breaking his rules for what she either should do or not do.

And finally, if he was angering at life or some life condition, then life was not up to par with his dictatorial master plan.

Whenever I work with angering, I'm looking to identify the main context or contexts where the person is angering. Tom had two typical situations. One was when he was attempting to bring up a certain topic and his wife rolled her eyes and stonewalled him. The other context was when she criticized him.

> **Jørgen:** "Let's be honest here. Do you merely prefer that she not criticize you, or do you demand that she must not? You see it's not her criticizing you or rolling her eyes that 'make you angry'. It's that she criticizes you while you absolutistically, inside your own head, demand that she must not do so."

Tom blushed slightly and started to get it.

> **Jørgen:** "So god demands that his worshippers do not have other gods than him. You demand that your wife must not criticize you. That and that you *need* her to listen and that she absolutely *should* not roll her eyes at you. Those are the commandments, and that's your religion. You're a religious nutcase."

That was essentially all it took for him to have his big light bulb moment. To help reinforce his insight we did a symptom prescription format I have developed.

Here are the steps of prescribing Musturbation.

1. Identify strong context.

2. Identify the internal musturbatory demand that the client is making.

3. Access state by either remembering a past event or imagining a similar one in the future.

(Tom imagined being back at a recent event where his wife criticized him.)

Use your congruence, intent, suggestions and embedded commands to help a person associate fully into the experience. Make sure the client's breathing pattern, facial expression and other physiology is congruent with state. Also make sure your own state is congruent with the responses you want to evoke. Instruct your client to make pictures bigger and brighter.

4. Measure state. Ask the client how strong the feeling is on a scale from one to ten.

5. Have the client deliberately musturbate. Have him internally tell himself that his wife must not criticize, etc. This will almost always intensify the experience. You can help the client along by suggesting: Notice that the stronger you *demand* (whatever they are demanding) the more intense the feeling.

6. Once you calibrate that you have gotten as intense a state as you can get, have the client measure the feeling again. Almost without exception, the feeling will have gotten stronger.

This is key as it helps the person have a felt experience of how musturbating increases their misery.

7. Immediately instruct the client to say to himself the word "Bullshit!", then imagine stepping out of his body so that he can, from a distance, see himself over there in that situation.

8. Then have him imagine that the musturbatory demand is a lens or pair of sunglasses that he has been viewing the world through. Suggest he remove the lens and place it in front of him so that he can begin to look at it. Now that the internal demand has been symbolized outside of him, ask the client questions designed to challenge and dispute the absolutism—questions such as, "Is there some law in the universe that says that she must not criticize you...or is it a wish and preference inside your head?"

You will see a solid state shift as soon as he questions his own horse shit and realizes that it is not true.

9. Have the client step back into the context, with a new running commentary in the back of his head, something like, "I would really prefer if my wife didn't criticize me, but there is no damn law in the universe that says that she absolutely shouldn't." Use your skills with hypnotic language patterns and suggestions to help them notice how their felt experience changes as they only strongly prefer X, and at the same time realize that they don't *need* for it to be so.

10. As soon as you can calibrate that there has been a solid shift in state, ask the person to rate the feeling once again if necessary, keep repeating step 10 until you get as low as 3 to 0.

11. Ask what they experienced and what insights they made while doing the exercise, and have them verbalize it. It's important that they "get" that they are "feeling their musturbation", and that they also have the experience that once they no longer believe in their musturbatory demand the feeling radically shifts. Otherwise they may turn their feelings up and down in the office and credit you or

the technique itself with making them feel differently. The highly hypnotizable client may have a dramatic shift in state in the office due to internalizing the suggestions, and still be as neurotic when they step into a perceived "problem" context.

Once again, the client gets another strongly felt experience of how their thinking influences how they feel. This time he experientially discovers that by wanting and preferring, as opposed to musturbating, rage and angering turns into merely irritation and annoyance or shifts into a state of calm. Anxiety and panic shifts into concern, or the feeling quite simply vanishes.

I usually repeat the whole sequence one or two times. Then I have the client do the whole sequence on their own. Usually, the client is instructed to prescribe their musturbating this way a couple of times a day until our next session.

This is the pattern I used with Tom, and he made very good use of it.

Alongside the affect bridge hypnotic "regression" work described in my previous book, *Provocative Hypnosis*, this is my bread and butter stuff.

This way of working has a tendency to accomplish some really neat results, as it helps people apply musturbatory ideas to philosophies such as, "I must succeed...I need to be respected and loved...my life should be exactly the way I want it and not offer too many frustrations." These irrational musturbatory philosophies contribute to a lot of anxiety, anger issues and depression and seem nearly universal. While a lot of people do obscene amounts of musturbation and others do relatively little, it's quite a challenge to find someone who does not engage in it at all. As far as I know I haven't met anyone and that includes me. These beliefs run people's lives as they have a tendency to view life *through* them.

41

When we view life through some deep assumption, that assumption *has us*, and we don't have any choice about it. By making the musturbatory philosophy conscious we can begin to look at it and *have* it, versus being had *by* it. This opens up a truckload of choice and contributes to people being a hell of a lot less neurotic.

INFORMATION VS TRANSFORMATION

It is useful to differentiate between in-form-ation and transform-ation. In-form-ation is essentially about new strategies, perspectives and knowledge that fit into a person's current way of meaning-making/form. Trans-form-ation, on the other hand, is about updating and changing the form, the way of understanding the person knows, understands and perceives through. By helping someone take some belief, deep assumption, etc., that has had them, that they have looked at the world *through* and turning it into something they can look *at*, you are helping them relativize (and therefore have choice about) something that was absolute.

Albert Ellis discovered that his clients' irrational beliefs/demands could be put into three categories. In my experience he is right about this, and it offers a very useful road map.

1. I must succeed.

2. I need to be respected.

3. Life and the world should behave the way I dictate.

This demand could be about having to get good grades, winning a tournament, having complete integrity in relation to internal standards, having control over own internal state, etc. To top it off, people then usually rate their own "essence" or self as good or bad, depending on whether or not they have met this demand.

This is a great recipe for feeling anxious and shameful.

43

One perverse consequence of this line of thinking is that even if people succeed they have a tendency to anxietize and self-anger just as strongly. Sometimes they even increase their own neuroticism, then depress themselves.

I have had many clients who are stuck in this kind of neurotic bind. Demanding that they "must succeed" creates anxiety and contributes to a lot of people either sitting on the sidelines or plunging forward with unnecessary anxiety. But succeeding doesn't help with anxiety as long as the person keeps up his irrational musturbating.

James, a former client of mine, was a great example of this. He had recently enjoyed some huge career breakthroughs. A heavy musturbator, he experienced a boost of temporary happiness. He had sincerely believed that once he had reached those career breakthroughs he would be happy and have great self-esteem. While he was happier for a while, he was stunned when his happiness levels returned to normal and his anxiety habit remained as strong as ever. He went into a deep depression.

Think about it—what internal demands is he likely making? He had a belief that said that if he couldn't be happy now, then he would never be happy. Not that strange considering his strong belief that achieving certain career goals would provide the happiness and feeling of being "good enough" that he so desperately demanded.

The internal demand was "*I should be profoundly happy now*". Anyone who is strongly shoulding that he should be happy right now—and simultaneously discovers that he isn't all that happy—will experience misery.

I did two things to help James. The first piece was information based—teaching him about research done on happiness and providing him with some new approaches and strategies. Also telling him stories about how lottery winners and victims of accidents both have a tendency to revert back to their baseline happiness well within a year. We humans through habituation have a tendency to overestimate the impact of significant life events when it comes to long-term happiness.

In this way he could see that his expectation was unrealistic and that the limitations/strengths of habituation were not a personal flaw but a tendency of human nature.

The more transformational part came when we used the exact same musturbation symptom prescription format as previously described. I had him get in touch with his gloomy feeling. Then he was instructed to go inside his head, demand that "*I should be happy now*" and to rate himself as a "fuck-up" while simultaneously feeling his gloomy feelings. Not too surprisingly, his gloomy feelings got stronger and stronger. Once he rated the feeling at a 9 on the 1–10 scale, I had him congruently say the word *bullshit* on the inside followed by imaging the demand as a pair of glasses he put at arm's length in front of him. James worked hard at questioning the *should* statement and showed a strong visible state shift when he realized that it was just an idea. He then practiced telling himself congruently that he wanted to be happy and that it was utter bullshit that he somehow *should* be happy when he wasn't. He also practiced thinking that the idea that he as a person/his essence could be either "good enough" or "fucked up/not enough" was sheer nonsense, and that instead he could regard his thinking as useful or not.

Some people may be surprised to hear that this intervention plus continued practice not only stopped his depressing, but did way more to boost his long term happiness than his external achievements had ever done.

A Miserable Architecture Student

John was a student of architecture who had recently begun to strongly depress. He felt drained of energy, sad. He experienced life, and especially his studies, as hopeless and meaningless.

John had previously been obsessed about being at the top of his class. Hard-working, conscientious, ambitious and a heavy musturbator. Then one day, seemingly out of the blue (to those around him), he did a 180-degree shift. Now it was all meaningless.

When this happens, more often than not, what has *not* changed is that the person is internally demanding that he must succeed. When someone is engaging in absolutistic thinking then it's natural for things to be very either/or. A lot of people (but certainly not all) who claim to have no motivation or goals are heavy musturbators who have "given up". They are often folks who have compulsively demanded a lot of themselves, but then realized that they won't get there. As a protective mechanism they then do a 180-degree shift.

This was the case with John. Due to a combination of factors, he realized that he would not become top in his class but remained a religious nutcase in his thinking.

I questioned him about what his greatest fears were if he imagined doing the opposite of what he was now doing (lying in bed, mostly). He discovered that he had a competing demand—he was afraid to discover that he wasn't as talented as he thought he was. He insisted that if that were the case, he couldn't handle it. It would also mean that he wasn't "good enough".

We did some work exploring these ideas and the short-term results seemed moderate. Unfortunately, I have no long-term feedback.

Over the years I have had many clients similar to John. Another common and very similar consequence of demanding success is that some clients may increase their performance anxiety right after an initial breakthrough result.

If the clients keep musturbating they are likely to think

something along these lines: My last presentation went great. Now everyone knows I can do it and they're going to expect me to be even better. I must be even better next time.

MRS. BUSH

Don't accept labels of "genius" or "miracle worker" from your clients. It's seductive for your ego but quite a trap, especially with a client who engages in musturbation.

See, if the client puts either you or your method on a pedestal, it often takes just one solid counter example for you to be a total fraud and for your method to be a huge disappointment. Early success becomes something that seemed promising, but "just didn't work". And the more the client massages your ego and credits you with the results, the less responsibility they will take when the shit hits the fan. It's a natural extension of perfectionistic either/or thinking.

Martha experienced a one-session resolution of several phobias in my office. Real-life testing confirmed our success.

About six months later she called me. It had taken her a few weeks to get herself to call. After our work together she had been convinced that her phobicking was completely gone. She told me so.

Then a few months later, at her hair dresser, she had begun to feel fear and panicked. Everything went downhill from there, and she concluded that it was all for nothing and completely hopeless. Another example of how people who engage in perfectionistic either/or thinking easily can do a 180-degree shift.

By the way, at the start of our conversation, I gave her a nickname of Mrs. Bush. I knew she was not a Republican, so calling her Mrs. Bush and teasing her about her either/or—you're either with us or against us—it's either fantastic or for nothing at all—hit home.

Our continued conversation, back at the office, went something like this.

> **Jørgen:** So it started back in the hairdresser's chair...as you sit there and you begin to *feel that feeling*...how do you know that you feel that feeling...*now* (Martha accesses state).... What's the first signal you get from your body...that lets you know...there comes the Fear...point to where you *feel that feeling*.

> **Martha:** It starts in my tummy (self-gestures).

At this point I point to where she's gesturing and say: There *you feel that feeling*. Marking out the sentence that way works both as an embedded command and an anchor. My pointing to where she is gesturing as she feels it also provides a visual anchor.

> **Jørgen:** As the feelings grow more intense...notice where it spreads.

> **Martha:** My heart is beating and my mouth is dry.

> **Jørgen:** On a scale from one to ten, how *intense* is that feeling *now*?

> **Martha:** Five

> **Jørgen:** As it gets even stronger now...inside, think "I must not feel this. I *must* not feel this. Oh my god, it's horrible. I can't stand it!"

Martha gets into it and is panicking, trembling and hyperventilating.

> **Jørgen:** How strong is it now?

Martha: Ten. (She is obviously a good hypnotic subject.)

Jørgen: Say the word *bullshit* and step out of your body at the hairdresser's chair...so that you can see *her*...having that experience over *there*.

Already here there is a marked reduction in her state.

Then I had her dispute the idea that she must not feel that way...and that she can't handle it, and that it's all for nothing.

I then instruct Martha to explore re-entering the hairdresser's chair and think: "I would like to feel calm, but I don't have to...and I can handle feeling whatever I feel."

It didn't take long for her feeling to be back at zero.

After a short break I looked at her intently and said: You know what it's like when you begin to (I point at her tummy) *feel that feeling*.

She is right back into the state. We repeat the rest of the sequence. Then I suggest that if she touch her tummy and think *"feel that feeling"*, she will access the state by herself.

Teaching a client to *have* a relapse or retriggering of symptoms versus being *had* by them is easily accomplished this way. Another thing that's great with this format is that if, in the future, she were to access the feeling, her brain knows that a strong *"Bullshit!"* to jolt her out of it, combined with disputing, is the next step after musturbating about the whole thing.

If you're working with a state itself that's not associated with any particular context, then what I did with Martha works wonders (most of the time).

Evoke the state using intent, indirect and direct suggestions and embedded commands. Notice and echo their spontaneous self-anchor (gesture/self-touch) and say *"Feel that feeling"* while you point to where they pointed. It can help to simultaneously touch yourself in the same way. Then do

49

the rest of the format as described earlier, i.e. "I must not feel this", "I can't stand it", etc. Later you can just fire off the anchors to get the feeling started. Then, so that the person can symptom prescribe on their own, you can suggest that all they have to do to access the state is to fire self-anchor and think, *"Feel that feeling."*

That approach is great for folks with some hypnotic capacity.

Let me give you a couple of practical approaches for the left-brained "I must not feel this" musturbators.

I prefer to use a formula I have borrowed from the meditation teacher Shinzen Young.

Namely that *a symptom is thoughts, feelings and body sensations plus resistance.*

Some internal representation comes up and we resist it. The resistance takes the form of fixation where we obsess and spin stories. The other form of resistance (one does not exclude the other) is by fighting it, tensing, and demanding that the thought/feeling not be there. The last one is extremely common with the left-brainers.

One solution, if they cannot access the feelings deliberately or through hypnosis, is a symptom prescription.

Let's say the client scares himself when it comes to public speaking. Simply, after establishing the devil's pact, task them with utilizing their symptom to connect to their audience when they introduce themselves. Usually I task my left-brainers with saying something like this: I can feel my pulse beating...my heart is racing...it's quite exciting here... but let me tell you...what's really exciting is X (whatever the topic is).

This principle of utilization can be used in so many creative and functional ways.

I highly recommend going through all the books written

50

by and about Milton Erickson. The guy's ability to combine observation, utilization and strategic thinking is as legendary as his contribution to hypnosis.

You can also take a client out in the world and utilize his problem as a bridge to create a solution. One young man—who was ruminating excessively, on the verge of suicide, and unable to speak to women—could only be helped this way.

Nothing happened in my office, so I suggested we hit the streets so that he could speak to some women.

"But I don't know what to say!" was his intense battle cry. So I dragged him out of the office and went up to a few women myself. I told them that my friend and I were talking about how neither one of us were quite sure how to initiate a conversation with a random stranger...and how would *they* do it?

Some walked past me, others stopped and offered their opinion and perspectives.

Then my client did the same. Even though he thought he was going to have a heart attack, he survived. One of the women even found the question intriguing, engaged in quite a bit of conversation, and even asked him a couple of questions.

Our work together—the constructive parts—consisted of skill building through behavioral tasking and using written exercises to challenge his musturbation and self-rating. The results were not that impressive—somewhere between mild and moderate reduction of his depressive symptoms. And when last heard from he had been on a couple of dates.

STANLEY SCHACHTER'S DISCOVERY

Paul Ekman documented how the 43 muscles of the human face combine to produce thousands of expressions, and how the human face has universal micro expressions for several different emotions. Along the same lines of thinking (presumably), psychologists attempted to identify the exact patterning of body sensations correlated with various emotions. There was one major obstacle, though. Although people experienced a wide variety of emotions, the body sensations that went along with these emotions seemed nearly identical. Many emotions and way too few distinct body sensations. How could this be?

A psychologist by the name of Stanley Schachter designed some brilliant experiments that turned conventional thinking upside down.

In one classic experiment participants were duped into thinking that they were part of an experiment that set out to test the effect of the drug suproxin (a nonexistent drug) on vision.

At the lab they were injected with suproxin (or so they were told). In reality they were given a shot of adrenaline. After being told that it would take some time before the shot took effect, they were escorted to a waiting room where they met another chap waiting for the effect of suproxin to take place.

Shortly thereafter the other guy started acting euphoric. Within fifteen minutes or so the participants were asked to report the effects of suproxin on their own bodies. People noticed their own beating heart and concluded that they too were euphoric.

Interestingly, when people were exposed to a fellow participant who acted angry, they interpreted the exact same body sensations to mean that they were angry too.

Schachter's theory is that the body sensations associated with every emotion are the same, but that we use context to interpret which emotion we are feeling—that there is simply one system that varies in intensity. On the one hand, when our physiology is activated, our pulse and heart rate goes up, we get warmer, our palms get sweaty and our mouth dries. We may tremble and experience butterflies in our stomachs. When you rest and relax, the system moves towards the other side of the spectrum with slower heart rate and lower pulse, etc.

Let's say you experience some butterflies in your stomach and a marked increase in heartbeat and you experience it while seeing an attractive woman. You are likely to interpret the body sensations as a sign of attraction. However, if someone you don't like throws an insult your way and you become aware of your increased heart rate and shortness of breath, you are likely to conclude that you're angry. In the roller coaster or before an athletic competition the exact same body sensations are probably going to be labeled nervousness or excitement. A sudden onset of the same body sensations on a plane, or in a tunnel, easily gets put into the phobic or panic category.

There are quite a few experiments that show that good old Stanley was on to something big.

Consider how violence and aggression has a tendency to go up as the temperature gets hotter. It's one thing to be walking on a beach, feel your pulse and increased body warmth, and then attribute it to walking on the beach in hot weather. However in a different context, a sudden increase in body warmth and pulse could influence people to interpret the body sensations as anger and act accordingly.

One group of researchers experimented with turning the heat up in their lab while participants were giving each other electric shocks to test the effect of punishment on learning. Quite predictably, a much hotter lab inspired participants to administer way more punishment. Feeling those body sensations while observing someone making mistakes got people to misattribute those sensations as evidence that they were

53

angry with the other person. After being given the opportunity to cool down with some cold water, people's aggression plummeted.

The perhaps most fascinating study (and most widely cited) was one done by Donald Dutton and Arthur Aron. They had a "market researcher" (a hot chick) approach men on two very different bridges across the Capilano River in British Columbia. One bridge was super solid. The other one was safe, but swayed enough with the wind to cause the men's hearts to beat faster. The "market researcher" approached the men to talk about some cause and handed them a brochure. At the end of her approach she gave them her card and invited the men to call if they wanted to talk more.

Not too hard to imagine what happened if you have read along so far.

The men in the second group (swaying with the wind) not only found her more attractive, they were also more than twice as likely to call her.

Just as with those who as a result of a warmer lab misattributed their increased heartbeat and body warmth to be anger, the men misattributed their own body sensations. The increased heartbeat, adrenalin, butterflies that they naturally felt on the "shaky bridge" were now interpreted as a strong attraction towards the market researcher.

I highly recommend that you purchase Richard Wiseman's book *The As If Principle*, for more examples of this topic.

Let's get back to the "I must not feel X" musturbators. Especially those who can't access X state through imagination or hypnosis in the office.

I will often tell them quite a few stories like the ones I have shared with you.

One client resolved his claustrophobia through insight by really "getting" this way of looking at emotion. He had suddenly had a panic attack after rushing, in very hot, humid weather, to reach a flight. Not long after takeoff he experienced sweating and a strong heartbeat. He noticed that his body was "trapped" between two other passengers while simultaneously becoming aware of these sensations and panicked. The more he tensed up and fought the "fear", the stronger it got.

His eureka moment, in my office, came when he realized that the whole thing was a case of misattribution of body sensations.

Another man, a high-powered CEO, came in with an anger issue. He said that he had no problems at work, but often just lost it as soon as he came home and one of his teenage sons mouthed off a bit. His rage, almost without exception, occurred on days of long hours at the office. I talked to him a bit about how we usually spend quite a bit of time every day fighting our own impulses so that we can be professional and stay in "control". And that will power is a bit like a muscle—it gets tired. This is "why" few people binge on ice cream or chocolate in the morning. Hence it was tougher to deal with two teenagers at the end of a twelve-hour work shift.

He realized that he had also tricked himself with a serious case of misattribution of body sensations. Rushing home while warm and sweaty (he worked five minutes away from home, so walked to and from work) with a high pulse, and becoming aware of those sensations while hearing some supposed insult or challenge to his authority, made his brain automatically conclude that he was royally pissed off, much like the sadists in the heated lab.

The following pattern helped both these guys (and many others).

1. Ask client to describe what happens in their body when

55

they feel their fear or anger. How do they know that they feel X? (The clients do not have to access those sensations while describing them, but it's a benefit if they do.)

Usually clients will talk about beating hearts, increased pulse, warmth, trembling, tingling, dry mouth and sweaty palms.

2. Have the client run on the spot intensely for about thirty seconds. Any hard physical exercise will do.

3. Then have the client stop, close their eyes, focus inward, and describe in detail what's happening in their body moment by moment.

Make sure they aren't analyzing. You're not looking for them to talk *about* what they are experiencing by saying they feel good or bad, or that they like it or don't. You want them instead to speak from their experience. An example would be, "A warm sensation is moving like a wave from my solar plexus to my lower lip...my stomach is buzzing in a clockwise direction...", etc.

With some luck they will have a big *"Aha!"* experience then and there. Often they experience the exact same sensations that they previously labeled anger or fear. You can also probe for it by asking: "...and your hands...your mouth...", etc.

4. Have them self-apply and practice describing their experience while moving along with their eyes open.

Here is a key skill/insight that I'm looking for them to have: to be able to experience a high pulse, increased heartbeat, etc., and to let it be *just* a beating heart or high pulse, etc., without labeling it "fear" or "anger" and going into their story.

What usually happens is that people feel some of the body sensations and then, more or less simultaneously, begin to go into their story. The story usually consists of images, internal dialogue and subtle thoughts. The images may increase the pulse rate, which may kick the internal dialogue into over-drive, etc. Like members of a vicious teenage gang, the various interdependent variables of the symptom loop mutually reinforce each other. It's a bit like a hypnotic loop where every part of a process strengthens and intensifies some hypnotic phenomena (more on hypnotic loops later).

A usual story in the symptom loop is the "I must not feel this" internal dialogue/increase of body sensations dance.

Another classic is: the "what if" game. The "what if" game is typical with anxiety, panic attacks and asthma. The person may feel her heart rate increase and then she thinks, "Oh my god...what if it's a panic attack...what if I faint...?" The heart rate increases, followed by another what if: "What if I lose it?" and they start hyperventilating, and on and on it goes.

Optional

5. Whether they symptom loop by practicing "I must not feel X" or by "what if-ing", have them deliberately do it.

Example: With their pulse high, after running on the spot, have them use internal dialogue and images to deliberately loop. Then after each "what if" have them label each component "dialogue", "image", etc.

The key skill that they are developing here is the ability to separate the body sensations from the story loop that goes along with it. Shinzen Young's teachings have been valuable here.

Sometimes the client's issue will completely resolve itself when doing this. At other times, their "stuff" may come back into play when they are, say, on the plane, but now the chances are that they can just have a beating heart for a little, without it being anything more than a beating heart. If, while on the plane, they can separate the body sensations from the story, they won't panic. And it won't take that long before they calm down since you need to fight or buy into the story for the symptom loop to get really strong and maintain itself.

Separate the sensations from the story and the sensations will change rather soon. It's a paradoxical approach. Don't attempt to change anything, but instead accept the experience so that it will change.

THE RAGING AUTHOR

Rebecca was an author, in her late thirties, who struggled with rage. Her raging tendencies were mostly directed towards her husband. As a goal-oriented woman with high standards, she had a tendency to be a perfectionist, controlling and somewhat compulsive about things. Whenever her kids and especially her husband didn't comply with her strict standards and rules, all hell would break loose. This happened especially if she was tired and stressed, which was often due to her schedule and compulsive tendencies.

This was many years ago and before I was aware of the work of Albert Ellis and his system of Rational Emotive Behavior Therapy. At that time I was a strict NLP- and hypnosis-oriented agent of change.

My approach was primarily state based. She was good at absorption and a decent hypnotic subject. Among the things we did was affect bridge regression and re-imprinting, as well as various anchoring formats where we would anchor resource states to her usual rage triggers and contexts. It all worked more or less brilliantly, at least for a while, but within a matter of weeks or months she would be back to her raging tendencies. After the new code change format (anchoring high-performance state to context) fared the same way, we did an interesting adaptation. Setting up involuntary signals with her unconscious, we negotiated a deal with her unconscious that recognized that there was a positive intention behind the raging. And that when we anchored a high-performance state to the context, the new ways of behaving based on the state would be in alignment with the original intent of her raging habit.

For those of you familiar with both classic code and new code NLP, you will recognize this as a combination of new code change format and six-step reframing. An intervention where the unconscious would be responsible for both the state/states linked to the old visual and auditory triggers of "problem" context, as well as for selecting behaviors in alignment with original intent behind the raging. Both of these patterns, as well as instructions for how to combine them, I have gotten from John Grinder. This also worked brilliantly, but unfortunately only on a temporary basis.

I decided on a very different approach. I had her write down the demands and standards she was compulsively imposing on her kids and husband. Once the demands were written down on paper (*my husband should exercise more*, etc.). I asked her four questions:

1. Is it true?

2. Can you absolutely know that it's true?

3. How do you react when you believe that thought?

4. Who would you be without that thought?

Rebecca had several eureka moments. There was a huge sense of relief when she had a felt experience of her demands being just thoughts.

This line of enquiring helps people explore their thinking and to realize that thoughts are just thoughts. She was then given turnaround questions. Let's take "he shouldn't watch so much TV".

1. He should watch that much TV.

She realized that he should be watching exactly the amount of TV that he was watching until he didn't, in the same way that it should be raining outside when it's raining outside—that's just the reality of it. People who depress over the weather by demanding "the rain should stop" and then blame the rain for their sad feelings often realize, through this question/turnaround, that it is them buying into and demanding "the rain should stop" while it keeps raining that generates the sad feelings

2. I shouldn't watch that much TV.

Rebecca quickly responded with pointing out that she hardly watched TV.

I then asked: "How about mentally? How often do you watch TV in your mind by picturing him in front of the TV screen while simultaneously telling yourself that he shouldn't do that?"

She realized that in a way she was watching even more TV than he was. While he was content with watching TV while he was watching TV, she did not restrict her mental TV watching to when she was watching TV.

The beauty of these turnaround questions is that they help people experience the opposite of what they have believed. Those of you familiar with the work of Byron Katie will hopefully have had that experience as well as knowing that Byron Katie's "The Work" was what I used with Rebecca.

Rebecca had a huge breakthrough that began when we went through her demands at my office. It continued when she read one of Katie's books (*Loving What Is*). This time the results were long lasting. She even went to the States to take part in one of Katie's courses.

More on Byron Katie and her method in the chapter on mind absolutism.

This experience was something of a wake-up call for me. It was the first of many cases where I discovered that it is often a lot more useful to help some clients to explore and dispute their absolutistic thinking, than it is to do more NLP-style sub-modality, anchoring and adjusting physiology/change your state-style interventions.

Combining the two (philosophy/state) gives even more bang for the buck, and the artistry often lies in knowing which aspect to emphasize.

The main point I'm making is that as long as people think that they *must* succeed, *need* to be liked, and absolutely *should* have the life they want, then they are likely to be a lot more neurotic than they would have been otherwise. This applies even when they achieve most of their goals.

My observation is that the combination of NLP patterning and musturbatory dogmatic thinking can be an express ticket into a whole new world of emotional pain. Far too many NLP trainers market absolutistic nonsense like: Have *total* state control, *always* get agreement, achieve rapport instantly with *anyone,* etc.

The main problem is that it just isn't true. You will never achieve total state control and you won't succeed with all your clients, even if you get damn good. Neither will you get hypnosis and hypnotic phenomena with all your clients, no matter how congruent and skilled you are. And despite Richard Bandler's claim of never *not* succeeding with a phobia client, you will find quite a few clients who won't respond to V-K dissociation or the famous NLP phobia cure. So has Bandler. On YouTube there is a clip where he does not succeed with a claustrophobic woman. Once, at a seminar, he did his spinning feelings technique with a woman who struggled with fear of public speaking. It looked impressive on stage, and he passed it off as a success, but when I asked her about it a few days later, there had been no change at all.

Encouraging absolutistic thinking through marketing hype combined with powerful NLP patterning will often result in NLP trainers who maintain their neuroticism as long as the dogmatic thinking continues. Someone who discovers that he still doesn't have total state control, and who simultaneously believes that he really should be able to control his state now that he knows NLP, can end up depressed, cynical and disillusioned. I have seen this way too often. If people keep rating their essence or self it can get ugly. One common consequence is that many of them amp up their denial, glibness and cognitive dissonance to attempt to convince themselves and others that their lives and relationships are perfect.

I have raised these concerns a few times with John Grinder. His observations are somewhat different from mine. His experience is that people's beliefs and absolutistic thinking will change automatically as soon as someone changes their state and connects a high-performance state to some context.

He is of course correct as far as it goes. And how far does it go?

I have had hundreds of phobia clients who have changed completely through state-based interventions.

This has, in my experience, been true with many of my clients with issues such as traumatic memories, migraine headaches, compulsions, chronic pain, depression, allergies, etc.

Often working with slight shifts of physiology can work wonders in shifting both state and thinking patterns. One consistent example for me, which has often been life-changing, has been working with stutterers. I will usually notice the person's breathing pattern when he or she is speaking fluently, as well as noticing how it is when the person is stuttering.

Making the person aware of those two distinct breathing

patterns is often quite a revelation.

By anchoring the fluent breathing pattern, by using my hands on the person's stomach to "pump the breathing" while he or she speaks on the phone (if that was a situation where they used to stutter) they experience speaking fluently. No, not always, but damned often. Then they learn to use their own hand to "pump" their breathing.

This is as pure a state intervention that you can get. And with stutterers, this intervention has usually been more useful than directly challenging their philosophical outlook. Full credit for this pattern goes to John Grinder.

Another interesting case was a young woman I worked with some years ago who had a schizophrenia diagnosis. She would often be tormented by an inner voice which instructed her to hurt herself and her son. The hallucinated voice scared the daylight out of her. Her experience was that the voice would just appear, without warning, out of the blue. My attempts at using indirect suggestion to evoke the voice was not successful. Having her deliberately imagine the voice didn't do any good as doing so didn't evoke any fear in her body. The real-time hallucination was as dramatically different from her conscious, deliberate, imagined voice as a hypnotic hallucination is in a whole different league of experience than someone just deliberately imagining something. In a case like this, REBT or the work of Byron Katie wouldn't have done much good.

So I did something different. I had her take her physiology into a state of fear, which didn't do much until I had her do the facial expression of fear (check Paul Ekman as a source of this). When she adopted the facial expression of fear and imagined the voice doing its thing she had a genuine fear response. Then I had her quickly place a pencil between her teeth, forcing a Duchenne smile—the Duchenne smile is a symmetrical smile where the muscles around the eyes are involved. She was further instructed to keep listening to the voice with the pencil-forced Duchenne smile while simultaneously shaking her head from side to side. Now the voice could say the same stuff as previously, but now she had the felt experience that it was silly. Most importantly, she had several undeniable experiences in my office that she could choose to buy in to the voice or not. This is another example of having an experience instead of being had by it.

Her homework symptom prescription exercise was designed to let her have the voice instead of being had by it. Right after deliberately triggering the fear/voice she jumped back while pushing her hands out in front of her and shouting "STOP!" This functioned to jolt her out of the fear state before she put the pencil between her teeth.

This helped her to do the exact same thing whenever the voice/fear came to visit, and to do so with less and less concern since she had experienced on several occasions that she could handle it.

While she was very happy with this for a while, she started to pretend that she couldn't help it and chose not to come back and do further work. I honestly don't know what competing commitments were occupying the dance floor inside her, and what factors in her social life that may have contributed to her decision, but that's life sometimes.

Having said all this, my experience is that challenging people's musturbatory philosophies is, more often than not, more useful than state-based intervention for some clients. This is especially so with people who struggle with anger issues, anxiety issues and depression as well as panic attacks. And it's useful irrespective of hypnotic capacity. The less capacity for absorption and hypnotizability, the more cognitive and behavioral approaches will have to be emphasized.

And there are plenty of counter-examples to Grinder's observation.

While many people's thinking patterns will change after a solid state-based intervention, there are plenty of clients like Rebecca out there—people who may temporarily change, but who won't make a long-term change until you help them modify their philosophical outlook.

Rebecca didn't change her compulsive musturbating no matter how many state shifts she made. Don't take for granted that your client will either.

The prescribing musturbating pattern combines the better of two worlds—NLP/hypnosis and REBT. I don't expect you to believe me when I say that it's way more effective, but I do expect that you set up experiments on your own to figure out if this is true.

Over the years I have come to the conclusion that NLP and REBT complement each other greatly.

For those see-feelers who are more action oriented, NLP and hypnosis often works better than REBT. However, for those left-brainers with poor access to feelings, who don't visualize well in conscious awareness, and who are prone to analysis and attempts at logical understanding while ruminating a lot using internal dialogue, REBT will probably work a lot better.

For some strange set of reasons the NLP and REBT worlds seem to pretend that the other party doesn't exist. Too bad. They have a lot to contribute to each other, and I recommend you explore both approaches.

65

JØRGEN RASMUSSEN

THE MYTH OF STATE CONTROL

Those who operate from a more self-authored mind, like Rebecca, no longer think that their emotions are directly caused by others' comments and actions. They realize that they largely create their own misery by how they *interpret* someone else's intentions and actions. So far, so good. However the self-authored clients, often on constant self-improvement projects, can delude themselves into thinking that they can (and should) be able to control their own thoughts and emotions.

Too often, NLP trainers will welcome the goal of 100% control over one's own thoughts and emotions and promise their clients that they can have total control of their own state. Sorry, Mac, it's bullshit. I have seen a number of alleged masters of state control (me included) completely lose it.

Whenever a client seems to think that they should have control over their own thoughts and emotions I will ask them the following questions:

1. If I were to claim that you breathe...is that true?

2. If I were to claim that you think, is that true?

I have never had anyone disagree with these two claims. Then I suggest that we turn the claims on their head.

3. You don't really breathe, you are being breathed.

4. You don't really think, rather you are being thought.

These claims usually elicit some confused clients. Some agree with claim 3 and almost no-one immediately agrees with claim 4.

While you can deliberately hyperventilate or choose consciously to take some deep breaths, if you didn't offer your breathing a single thought during the next twenty-four hours you will find that you are being breathed even while you sleep. The same goes for thinking. Although you can deliberately reflect, ask questions and consciously imagine various things, the same applies here. If you were to attempt to not have a single thought in the next twenty-four hours, you would never succeed.

Thoughts appear while you sleep and spontaneously arise in your waking state whether you want them to or not. You are being thought. In fact, you don't know what your next thought will be until you find yourself thinking it.

Reread the last sentence and consider the implications.

Since most of our thinking never reaches conscious awareness, and most of the thinking that does reach conscious awareness just spontaneously comes up, the idea that we can (and should) be in total control of our thinking is seriously flawed. The thought pops up, it's already happened, and then we chide ourselves for thinking it. But it's like a dog in constant pursuit of its own tail. That we can't control our thinking isn't really a problem. The problem lies in the taken-for-granted belief that one should, or even must, be able to do it, then in discovering again and again that one comes up short.

I do my best to persuade my clients to give up the idea of control. Having control presupposes a cause-effect relationship that is nonexistent. Instead I do my best to have them settle for having some *influence* over thoughts, feelings, state and modus. The main idea here is that while we don't have control we do (presumably) have at least some deliberate

67

choice and influence. Through NLP techniques, REBT and a solid meditation practice, we can learn to have even more choice and influence. We can transform our relationship to our own thoughts and feelings, resulting in us meeting them with more equanimity. This transformed relationship of presence and equanimity towards thought and feelings will alter both our automatic thinking and rewire our brain. There is plenty of scientific documentation on meditation practice in support of this.

THE NAZI PATH TO PERSONAL GROWTH

Both with private clients and seminar participants I often accuse them of being Nazis, even committed Nazis. Since I'm sincere when doing so, people often get a little uncomfortable and confused, enough to secure their full attention.

The barbaric ideology of National Socialism and its devoted followers were deeply committed to the so-called Aryan race. As long as you were of that race your essence as a human being was good.

There is no mercy or human worth in that ideology for any deviation. If you were a Jew, negro, homosexual or mentally retarded, the gas chambers were your destination.

Let's, in light of this, take a look at how many people think about self-improvement.

Somewhat arbitrarily, we use language to impose boundaries and categories on the flow of experience—boundaries and categories that make life appear much more fixed, organized and predictable than it really is. Good or bad, right or wrong, strong or vulnerable, etc. Then we act as if these linguistic constructs and boundaries are inherent in the flow of experience, instead of being mostly imposed on the flow of experience by language.

People will usually identify with one side of a polarity and call it "me" or who they are. As soon as they identify with one

69

side of a polarity, then the other side will automatically be a "not me". Then they rate their essence or overall self as good.

If a person identifies with being intelligent or a strong person, then stupidity or vulnerability will be threatening to their sense of self and result in anxiety.

You can learn a lot about how people make meaning, how they are selfing, and their deeper assumptions by discovering which dichotomies they operate out of.

Those who operate out of earlier stages of meaning-making (the self-sovereign mind) tend to be full of dichotomies and engage in a lot of black and white thinking. The few who operate from a self-transforming mind have a tendency to have very few, if any, dichotomies.

Where the self-sovereign mind operates with a strong either/or black and white thinking style where, say, intelligence and stupidity are distinct and a strong person is distinct from a weak or vulnerable person, the self-*transforming* mind uses a more both/and as well as an *and* logic. They see more shades of gray on a continuum influenced by contextual factors. They are more likely to see the strength in vulnerability, and the vulnerabilities in the way they conceptualize strength, in the same way that they can see the stupidity in intelligence and the intelligence in stupidity.

Anyway, with the exception of those who operate more from a self-transforming mind (the self-sovereign mind is not psychologically oriented) the socialized mind and the self-authored mind are often committed Nazis. They will have a tendency to take one aspect of a polarity—such as intelligent, compassionate, strong, certain—and identify with it.

Simultaneously, they do what they can to send all seemingly opposite sides of the pole (stupidity, selfishness, vulnerability and uncertainty) to the gas chamber. The tendency is usually even stronger with the socialized mind, which will engage in a lot of projection.

If you can help people uncover their dichotomies and guide them to think more in a both/and fashion where they used to have a strong either/or, you can likely be part of some serious shifts.

Let's take a look at a couple of case stories.

Jacob came into my office with the request of making permanent a change he was able to implement part of the time. He told me that he used to be terrified of public speaking.

He had been to a hypnotherapist/NLP practitioner who had been able to help him along the way. The hypnotherapist had instructed him to change his internal imagery. Jacob had previously made a picture of the audience staring at him with bulging eyes and unfriendly facial expressions. When he changed his internal picture into one where the audience had friendly eyes and smiling faces the fear disappeared and was replaced with a sense of confidence. Jacob had done better in front of his audience since seeing the hypnotherapist, but he was still very concerned and feared that the fear would come back. Jacob said that he had to picture the audience in a positive way and that he had to be a positive person. He didn't know if he could keep it up. He was fighting his negative thoughts so that he could remain a positive person.

The observant reader will have noticed the absolutistic thinking present when Jacob *had* to picture the audience a certain way. In addition to this we had the either/or dichotomy between positive and negative. There didn't seem to be any curiosity or awareness around how negativity could be a resource. There was no seeing the positive in the negative or vice versa. The icing on the cake was the identity statement of being a positive *person*.

71

My first objective was to find out "why" he would have to picture kind eyes and smiling faces in the audience so as not to feel fear in front of them.

Personally, if I imagine a hostile audience, it still doesn't trigger fear, so I know that it's not a given.

WANTING VS. WILLINGNESS

In the past, in light of my classic NLP training, I was very interested in what clients wanted. These days, it hardly matters to me. As soon as clients start rambling about what they want I have a tendency to stop them and say, "I don't care what you want—I only care of what you are willing to change or willing to work to learn how to change."

If you get a babbling client who talks about wanting a zillion things, throwing the willingness frame at them has a tendency to get them to "sober up" real fast and commit to one or a couple of things they really care about.

To set the frame, I tell my clients something along these lines: "Look, people want a lot of things. A lot of people may want to be really good at playing a sport or they might want to master an instrument, but that doesn't necessarily mean that they are willing to actually do what it takes.

"On the other hand, there are plenty of things that you may not want to do, like going to work on some days or doing the dishes after dinner, but despite *not* wanting to, you're still willing to do it."

The session with Jacob (and many others) progressed along the following lines:

> **Jørgen:** OK, let's imagine that you're in front of an audience and the worst happens. What's the worst that could happen?

Jacob: that my voice starts shaking, and that I lose control of my voice and panic.

Jørgen: Imagine that you're in front of an audience...only as quickly...as you begin...to connect with that *fear*...to the point where you *feel the fear*...in your body...now...as it get stronger...the more you focus in...the stronger it gets.

At this point, Jacob has gotten in touch with the fear. It's important for the "problem" state to be activated while I help him skate towards the edge of his map.

Jørgen: As you keep feeling the fear, Jacob... notice, as you imagine speaking, that sensation in your throat...that lets you know...you're losing control of your voice...and as you *really connect with that*...what is it about that that you fear the most?

Jacob: That people will think that I'm weak and look down on me (voice trembling).

Jørgen: So what...what's the worst about that?

Jacob: If I look weak and others think I'm weak, then I feel that I'm weak, unless I can make that positive picture.

Once we have skated up to the edge of the person's map— their deepest fear—it's time to ask the person if he or she is willing to have that experience.

Jørgen: As you keep feeling that...I imagine that your voice is failing you...the panic...how people think you're weak...to the point where you think you're weak...and no matter how hard you try, you can't picture the positive picture any more...how

74

strong is that fear in your body on a scale from one to ten?

Jacob: It's an eight.

Jørgen: OK, here is the big question: I know that you don't like that feeling, and that you really don't want to feel that feeling, but I'm asking you something different: Are you *willing* to have that experience?

Jacob: Yes... (visible state shift)

Jørgen: Notice *that feels different*. Where is the feeling on the scale now? (notice my careful choice of words, how I don't ask him how strong it is)

Jacob: It's a four.

This usually happens. Once someone decides that he is willing to have the experience, a marked shift in state usually occurs.

Jørgen: It's a four. Stay in the experience and notice what it's like as an audio tape plays in the back of your head that says, "I'm willing to have this experience..." and notice how *the experience changes* as you experience the willingness while noticing how *the feeling changes*.

It didn't take long before Jacob's feeling was a one!

The pattern is quite simple:

1. Frame want versus willingness.

2. Have client imagine being in context.

3. Access state (usually happens in step 2).

4. While state is active ask questions such as:

A. What's the worst that could happen?
B. What about that scares you the most?
C. How is that the worst that could happen?

Ask several times. Feed what the client is saying back at him or her until the client can't verbalize further.

5. Get the client to rate intensity of their experience on a one to ten scale.

6. Ask client if he or she is *willing* to have the experience (make sure client understands that you're not asking if he or she *wants* the experience).

7. As soon as client confirms that he or she is willing, help them notice the state shift. Have the client rate the experience again.

8. Help the client stay present with their simultaneous willingness and experience and have the client notice how that changes the experience. Help along with hypnotic language patterns. Keep going until you get as low a rating as you can get.

9. Rehearse and have client self-apply. Often it is useful to give this as a symptom prescription homework assignment.

Troubleshooting Tip

If the client answers that he or she is not willing to have the experience, point out that this means she is looking *through* an "I must not experience this" filter. Have her imagine taking the filter off, like a pair of sunglasses, so that she can look *at* it and ask if there really is some law in the universe that says that she must not have the experience and that she can't handle it.

Proceed as with the prescribing musturbation pattern.

Since I started playing with this pattern about a decade ago, it's become one of my bread and butter approaches. Quite often, it contributes to some rather generative changes across contexts and at least a nudge towards a more complex meaning-making system.

In Jacob's case we were able to help him get some perspective on both his formerly held demand of "I must not lose control of my voice" and others "must not think that I am weak".

The deeper assumption and way of selfing that seems to drive the system appears primarily to be a socialized mind. With this orientation he *is* his relationship. His sensed self is co-constructed in that his view of himself and how he perceives important others viewing him together form the base of his self. Hence, how he thinks others perceive him, in this case "if others think I am weak then I think I am weak" show a socialized mind at work.

There does seem to be some capacity for self-authorship going on as well. Jacob does have a felt experience of being able to "have the last word", deliberately shifting how he feels by changing the picture in his mind. Still, it's fragile, and it's based on being able to think of his audience as approving of him. So the emerging capacity for self-authorship seems to be in service of a socialized mind—a mid zone (most typical) of socialized and self-authored with the former being more dominant.

A person who was strongly self-authoring could still feel anxious with regards to public speaking, but the anxiety would be based in perceiving himself as not able to live up to his own internal standards for how well he should perform. He may have a self-concept built around being a competent and persuasive teacher and use his audience reaction as evidence of not having been as skilled as he thinks he should have been.

Knowledge regarding Kegan's model of adult meaning-making has been useful to me. It's resulted in better rapport as a result of being better able to pace the meaning-making system a client is operating out of. It provides a useful
road map for where the client is likely heading, and it helps
make it less likely that interventions will turn out to be anti-developmental. When working with someone you may, in
collaboration with the client, help resolve their symptom by
making them more functional *within* their current meaning-making system. Jacob might have been helped by discovering that people are unlikely to notice his anxiety, that people may think of him as courageous for speaking up despite
his fear, and that he can use his anxiety to connect better.
These types of solutions may well work and be a good fit for
a socialized mind.

You can also help someone like Jacob in a way that is
more developmental. By helping him to *have* relationships
instead of being *made up* by them. Helping him to develop
a sense of self that is differentiated and distinct from how
he thinks others may view him. Having him developing his
own definitions and standards as well as the ability to change
the interpretations and stories he makes up about what the
whole thing means. For someone who is self-authoring, it
might be inconvenient that someone else may perceive him
as weak, but he is not going to define himself as weak as a
direct consequence of perceiving that important others may
view him that way.

When someone operating out of a socialized mind says
"public speaking makes me anxious", they literally have the
felt experience of being that way. The person with a self-authored mind, on the other hand, no longer holds others responsible for his own emotional state, nor does he believe that
he "makes others happy". Others may perceive him a certain
way, but since he has a self distinct from his relationship and

important others' expectations, he can author different stories about what something means. One consequence of this is that he is less likely to attempt to manipulate others into changing based on the belief that they will have to change for him to feel better.

FUNCTIONAL CONFIDENCE

As Kegan has pointed out, it's really not appropriate to talk about self-esteem before someone is self-authoring.

The social mind has "other esteem"; there is no differentiated sense of self to esteem. Most books on the topic of self-esteem seem to be about other esteem. For a book about self-esteem, check out Nathaniel Branden's masterpiece, *The Six Pillars of Self-Esteem*. If you want a mind-boggling philosophical experience, read Branden's book followed by Albert Ellis's brilliant, *The Myth of Self-Esteem*, and see what you make of it.

While I don't think of self-esteem and confidence as being the same thing, Jacob seemed to do so. Essentially, he wanted certainty. He made a common mistake—he attempted to base all his internal security on *predictability*.

This is very common and typical when people say that as long as they know everyone, know how they will react and that they are perceived as competent, then they will manage.

A big problem with this is that all it takes is for unexpected stuff to happen, and all their "confidence" falls apart. Of course deep inside they know that they can never have the guaranteed predictability they think they must have. So no matter how competent or prepared they are, anxiety threatens to rear its ugly head at any time.

Also remember the positive versus negative either/or in Jacob's model of the world.

I had him divide a piece of paper in two, using a line. On

the left-hand side he was to exercise his negativity by writing down all the things that could go wrong. On the right hand side he was to develop positive responses. *However*, these positive responses were to be based not on predictability, but rather on *utilization*. Specifically, the question, "If X happens, how can I use it to present better and to connect better with my audience?" Then he was to write down a specific sentence/action to do for each point.

He was given an example of a public speaker I once heard who suddenly lost his train of thought on stage and forgot about what he was supposed to say. Instead of the common tactic of giving some pathetic excuse or rowing the boat of desperation, this guy did something quite different. He stopped, got real quiet, and then asked, "How many here have had something on the tip of your tongue...like you knew what you were going to say, but for some reason you just couldn't access it? If you ever had that experience, please raise your hand." Of course, since it's a near universal experience, all raised their hands. The speaker instructed everyone to look around while they kept their hands up and to realize that we were all in the same boat...since this was exactly what he was experiencing in this very moment. Could anyone tell him what on earth he had been talking about? The audience burst out laughing and it didn't take long before half the audience eagerly wanted to help him out.

The main point is this. While he was doing OK before his sudden onset of amnesia, he had a much better connection with the audience afterwards. He masterfully utilized his amnesia as a means to bond and connect with his audience.

Writing one's own definitions promotes self-authorship.

I'm happy to report that the work Jacob and I did together was very successful. The interventions both utilized his current way of meaning-making and also helped develop more self-authorship.

By the way, the writing exercise I gave Jacob has proved useful for many of my clients. Even fear of public speaking clients who are too "left-brained" to get in touch with their fear in the office have often resolved their issue just by doing the writing task. Combining it with the "running on the spot" pattern described previously is often a slam dunk. No absorption skills or hypnotic capacity required.

A CASE OF FLAWED PERFECTION

Lisa was a woman who struggled a bit with compulsive thinking as well as anxietizing herself in situations where she thought she had to perform. She also related to some social situations in a fearful way, especially situations where she felt she was viewed as incompetent.

Lisa was a control freak and very analytical. Trusting people was hard and letting go very difficult. She identified strongly with *being* a perfectionist. She told me that she demanded perfection of herself and that she was a compulsive perfectionist. Not surprisingly, she was scared to the core of making mistakes.

This dichotomy between perfection on one side and failure on the other appeared solid.

Since she had little, if any, hypnotic capacity to deliberately alter her own experience by using her imagination, we did not get anywhere when I attempted NLP- and hypnosis-oriented approaches. I gave her a discount for the first session and established a devil's pact with her before closing the session off.

It was time to hit the streets and utilize a combination of analytic and behavioral interventions to challenge her perfection-versus-mistakes dichotomy.

Lisa liked to dress well and was very aware of her image.

She was met with the following instructions and a specific challenge. She was to make a perfect mistake. Together we went to a gas station. She was instructed to buy a big bacon hot dog with ketchup and some other greasy stuff on it. Far away from her social image of classy and healthy eating. Then she was to make sure to have an "accident"—an "accident" of smearing herself with the greasy hot dog and dropping it to the floor, and do such a great job of it appearing to be spontaneous, that no-one at the gas station could see that the whole thing was well-planned and done on purpose.

Not only was the idea of a perfect mistake confusing to her, the whole task assignment seemed preposterous, and I think she started to question my sanity. However, with the devil's pact in place combined with Lisa being true to her word, she went along and did it.

It was a dramatic experience that pushed many of her buttons. She did, while very emotional, admit that she could handle it and that she had made a nearly perfect mistake.

Lisa was further instructed to plan and execute a perfect mistake in public every day for the following week.

The other task I gave her was just as confusing to her. She was to sit down with pen and paper and reflect upon the mistakes and shortcomings in the way she conceptualized perfection.

While I don't think she completely resolved her anxiety and compulsive perfectionism (I don't have long-term feedback) there were at least some moderate short-term improvements.

USING HYPNOTIC PHENOMENA
TO GET PERSPECTIVE

Stephen Gilligan has a saying, adapted from his studies with Milton Erikson, that I like a lot: "The problem is not the problem, rather it's that one perspective is being held in isolation from other truths and perspectives."

Quite often, the deliberate use of hypnotic phenomena is a great way to liberate frozen beliefs and perspectives.

In my previous book, *Provocative Hypnosis*, I gave many examples of using hypnotic phenomena in this way during a formal hypnotic process, after a hypnotic induction and in a context defined as a hypnotic one. I still sometimes work that way and it's a valid approach.

However, sometimes clients will give you something so precious, that you want to grab a hold to it right there and then and utilize a hypnotic phenomenon to help liberate some frozen belief or perspective.

Sometimes it's a lot more useful to go directly for hypnotic phenomena without either doing a pre-talk, or doing formal hypnotic induction or testing for somnambulism. Even skipping the whole hypnosis frame is often an advantage.

Since I often don't use formal hypnosis nor call myself a hypnotherapist, in much of my marketing I often don't use the term hypnosis. Instead I will often frame the whole thing up by asking, "Would you like to discover how you can have a lot more influence over (thoughts, feelings, your body, etc) than you may have thought possible up until now?" or, "Let's play an imagination game," or, "Let's do a mind experiment where you get to discover something interesting."

If we have great rapport I may just get into it with no set-up at all.

INSTANT ATTRACTION

I'm convinced that we resolved Sara's jealousy issue in a minute or so of actual change work time.

Sara would go ballistic if her boyfriend found another woman attractive. If he even looked at an attractive woman when Sara was with him, she would rage.

While this raging habit of hers was threatening her relationship, and she could see that she was irrational, that insight had no effect on her strong feelings of jealousy.

I probed for the most severe contexts and asked my typical: "What's worst about that? What is it about that that scares you the most?" questions. It didn't take long before she handed me her jealousy on a silver platter, saying, "If he finds other women attractive, that means he doesn't love me."

When she said this, she visibly went into her problem state. I told her the following:

> **Jørgen:** I just discovered how we can resolve your issue...you're going to change through an interesting mind experiment. Are you ready?

> **Sara:** Yes.

> **Jørgen:** Have you noticed how...when someone asks you a question....You can *feel* the answer to the question...and you find yourself *just respond automatically*...just like when you watch a movie...and something *exciting* happens...you automatically *feel the feelings*...that the characters

feel...in your body.... And it just happens automatically...?

Sara: *Yes*, I really get into movies.

The main reasons I do this setup is that it primes her by indirectly suggesting how she is to respond. I'm suggesting that I want her to respond automatically and with physical and emotional engagement. I do it by describing common examples of that type of responding, like being absorbed into a movie and responding emotionally to a question. I'm also emphasizing the dissociated "it just happens" aspect of these experiences. I'm lowering my voice tone and emphasizing words like *feel* and *excitement*. The state I'm going for right after this setup is attraction, so excitement is in the same ballpark. During this setup Sara demonstrated non-verbally that she was engaged and responding. Had she started to move around, fidget, or leaned back with a skeptical look on her face, that would have been a sign that she had gone into "left-brained" analytical mode.

> **Jørgen:** I'm going to make you fall in love with me and then make it disappear. Would you say that you love your boyfriend right now?
>
> **Sara:** Very highly.
>
> **Jørgen:** I don't know exactly what happens... when you begin to...*feel a strong attraction*... to the person in front of you (subtle self-gesture)... but when you...*feel attraction*... how do you know that...*you feel it now*...? What's the first thing that happens in your body that lets you know... *you feel it right now*.... Point to where the *feeling starts now*.

87

Sara: Butterflies in the stomach (her state shifts... starts breathing heavily).

Jørgen: And what's the next thing that happens in your body...as that feeling gets even stronger now?

Sara: Warmth spreads upwards...and my throat tightens.

Jørgen: Notice what it's like as those feelings reach their peak when you touch your face.

At this point Sara blushes.

Jørgen: On a scale from one to ten, how strong is that feeling of attraction you have towards me right now.

Sara: Nine.... Shit it's a ten. This is nuts!

Jørgen: Do you love your boyfriend?

Sara: *Yes.*

Jørgen: And you feel that strong attraction towards me...and you love your boyfriend?

Sara: *Yes.*

Jørgen: OK, notice what it's like as that attraction towards me goes away...to the point where... in a few seconds...your feelings towards me are back to neutral. Give me a nod when you're back to neutral.

Sara: Back to neutral (nods head).

Jørgen: And the big question is: Do you love your boyfriend?

Sara: *Yes.*

Sara bursts out laughing. She laughs so hard that tears are running down her cheeks, followed by utterances like, "That was *insane!*" and "What the hell did you do to me?"

> **Jørgen:** Me? I just asked some questions. What's the matter? Don't you love me anymore?

Sara starts laughing intensely again and says that she just went through one of the weirdest experiences she ever had.

Follow-up confirmed that her jealousy, and consequently rage, was completely resolved. She wrote a letter thanking me and wrote about how huge this change had been for her.

While some may think I was acting borderline unethical here (or way over the border), I'm pretty sure we were both OK with the whole thing.

The only thing I don't like about this particular intervention is that she left thinking that I did it to her—a view congruent with the socialized mind.

If you think so yourself, I would like to point out that I don't have direct control of her mind and that this was an experience we both had a part in creating. I presented her a frame/learning context based upon what she had given me. You could say that *we* created the learning context. After providing a context as well as offering suggestions, it made sense for her to respond the way she did.

She utilized her solid hypnotic capacity.

I've got to give credit where credit is due. While Milton Erickson pioneered the use of indirect suggestion and hypnosis, and John Grinder, Richard Bandler and Frank Pucelik spread Erickson's teaching through their NLP books and seminars, what I did here was heavily influenced by Paul Ross (formerly known as Ross Jeffries). Ross was the first guy to develop a system for seduction based on NLP. The way I evoked the feeling of attraction was based on Ross's work.

Whether you are interested in seduction or not (and who honestly isn't) I recommend checking out his work as it's very pragmatic, free of new-age clichés and political correctness.

Evoking feeling states in people in such a way that it's as if it's happening all by itself is probably the easiest hypnotic phenomena to elicit. For most people this will be true, even though some who are out of touch with their emotions may be better at other phenomena that many would find more difficult.

HYPNOTIC LOOPS

As previously mentioned, I often use Shinzen Young's formula: A symptom consists of thoughts and body sensations plus resistance. Some thought and/or body sensation/emotion comes up and we fight it by musturbating, "I must not feel this", etc., or we start "what if-ing". "What if I panic?" (pulse goes up) "What if I completely lose it?" (heart beats faster)...and then we may fight it, etc. Often the symptom loops have us in that they seemingly just happen, and attempts to control them often intensify the experience.

Imagination games and hypnotic loops can be used as metaphors as well as teaching tools for breaking the spell through symptom prescription.

BOOK AND BALLOON GAME

This is an old-school suggestibility test, and most who use it use it as such.

While I also use it to test for hypnotic capacity, I mostly use it as a teaching tool. Usually I frame it as an imagination game and say something to the effect of, "Would you like to discover the power of your imagination?"

This set-up is important. The discovery/active participant frame makes it less likely that they will view the whole thing as a battle of wills and attempt to prove their superiority by resisting.

After you have them stretch their arms out with one palm up and the other one down, the language goes something like this: "Imagine that I have a heavy book, like a *heavy* phone directory...and imagine me putting that *heavy* directory in *that* hand...and notice that the more you focus in on that *heavy* phone directory in *that* hand...the heavier and heavier it gets...as *that* arm begins moving downwards...as if it's happening all by itself.... And as that continues all by itself... imagine a bunch of helium balloons attached to *that* arm is lifting...lifting...*floating* lighter and lighter...as *that* arm goes *up* in the air now...."

That's pretty much it. Make sure to ratify every little move by saying "that's right" every time you get a response you want. There are many subtleties here that go into making this as effective as can be. Notice how I encourage dissociation by talking about *that* arm moving. You can pace the lifting suggestions with their in breath and the heavy directory suggestions with their out breath. If they respond better to, say, the lifting suggestions than the heaviness suggestions, you can chain them together and create a loop. Say something like, "And the more you find *that* arm lifts higher and higher the more you can feel the heaviness of that phone directory in *that* hand is dropping down all by itself."

Notice what I did in that last sentence, the use of ambiguity and confusion. By saying something like: "As you imagine me putting a heavy directory in *that* hand is getting *heavier*..." The slight confusion contributes to the responding to the next clear instruction. If they won't quite get going I usually use ambiguity and confusion to good effect.

Also, some may respond even better if you add imagining an empty bucket on top of the phone directory and have them imagine hearing the sound of water being poured into the bucket.

Finally, notice how I use the word "imagine" as a failsafe

general choice instead of "picture". If the client is good at visualizing in conscious awareness, then "picture" is great. However some people will claim that they can't make pictures, and you will easily lose them if you don't take that into account.

If you don't get much of a response, then in my experience the person either isn't following the instructions or they just don't have the ability to do it.

Sometimes all it takes is asking the person what they were doing internally. Often they are talking to themselves about the experience and engaging in thoughts like "What's the point of this?" or "What if it doesn't work?", etc. If that's what they're doing, then no wonder nothing much is happening. Simply invite the client to actually engage and do the experiment the next time.

If you still don't get a response, then going for a more behavioral-/cognitive-oriented approach will often be better than the hypnosis route.

There are exceptions, though. I remember a guy with massive asthmatic reactions based on a couple of allergies. When I did the phone directory and the balloon game his hands didn't move at all. I still went for a hand drop induction followed by an affect bridge "regression" using his symptom as a bridge. We got our one-session "miracle". Sometimes people can respond a hell of a lot better when you use their symptom as the entry point.

It goes to show you that there isn't a perfect correlation between test results for hypnotic capacity and how the person responds when they get engaged with their stuff.

UNBENDABLE ARM

Once a client is solidly engaged in the phone directory and balloon game, I will stretch one of her arms out and have her

"...imagine a steel bar going from your shoulder...through your elbow...to the wrist...making *that* arm is stiff and rigid..." (The slight use of confusion is to amplify experience.)

Then I suggest (after calibrating that she is engaged with the experience) that as soon as I touch her wrist her arm will get so stiff that the more she tries to bend it, the more she will find that it stays stiff and rigid.

Most people will have a solid experience of an unbendable arm at this point. Both the phone directory and balloon game and the unbendable arm are very convincing and impressive to most, and they're low-risk since most people can do them. These ideomotor "muscle suggestions", are in my experience, almost as easy to get with clients (in general) as evoking some feeling response through suggestion.

These games serve a couple of important functions in my work. I use them both as diagnostic tools (testing for hypnotic capacity) and metaphorical teaching tools. Here's how: After the games, I explain to clients that the exact same resource capacities that they discovered during the games are the ones they use to generate their symptoms.

First some thought appears, then that thought turns into a train of thought that they become absorbed into (such as the "what if" game of panicking on a plane), and then once it's "as real as real" they start to fight and resist the experience, which has a tendency to amplify it.

This is a eureka moment for many clients. At this point I will usually use a phrase that I have borrowed from a guy named Sydney Banks, who has become famous for his three principles approach to psychology. The saying is: You're living in the *feelings* of your thinking, not *what* you are thinking *about*. In other words, the client may engage in scary thoughts around being on a plane or speaking in public, then feeling their thinking in the same way when they think/imagine that they have a heavy book in one hand, and balloons attached to the other wrist. They get absorbed into it. They feel their thinking and their body responds as if it's real, despite there being no balloons, books or steel bars there.

The experience will be "as real as real" depending upon to what extent they engage and get absorbed into the suggested experience.

There is no doubt that people vary a lot in their capacity for getting absorbed into a suggested experience. Decades of hypnotizability testing have shown this to be true, and the findings are extremely stable over time.

While some will get completely absorbed into the suggested experiences, others will have more of a partial response—an "it was unbendable and I knew I could bend it at the same time" type of response. Someone might struggle a bit and then bend it. And someone could just bend their arm, roll their eyes, and give you a look of contempt. If they do so you have a golden opportunity to utilize it in a way that's likely to jolt them: "And *that* is exactly how you are going to eliminate your symptom. You just demonstrated that exact resource... the ability to treat thoughts as just thoughts...the ability to imagine and think something is real while simultaneously knowing that it's not."

Of course the "real as real" responses are even easier to utilize. You point out that they have an enormous ability to deliberately change their feelings and physiology by using their imagination, and that is exactly what they are doing when raging or doing anxiety.

You can offer to teach clients with high hypnotic capacity more about how to deliberately use that capacity to create different experiences, instead of being at its mercy. However it's just as important that they develop more choice about *not* getting absorbed into suggested experience, including their own automatic stuff. Highly hypnotizable folks have a tendency to slip into hypnotic states spontaneously and get absorbed into experiences. While absorbed, they may accept suggestions that "seemed like a good idea at the time" and later wonder how they could be so silly.

These folks, due to high capacity for absorption and dissociation, often experience their emotions as "just happening" and caused by others; hence, the importance of balance, of having choice about "going there" or not. The combination of high hypnotic capacity and a socialized mind seems extra risky. It's very likely that these factors are at play in cases of false confessions in the legal system, people who "discover" nonexistent sexual abuse through therapy, people who develop so-called multiple personalities and other more common symptoms as a result of suggestions in a psychotherapeutic or medical context.

It's important that those with little capacity for hypnosis orient inwards and become more aware of their internal world. In that way they can begin to use their skepticism applied to other's suggestions to have more choice about not buying into their internal symptom loops and fixed meanings. For the low-hypnotic-capacity group, often concerned with analysis and understanding, it's often useful to frame the process as one of learning how to de-hypnotize themselves out of automatic symptom loops and fixed meanings.

Anyway, back to the games. I will often have them go through the games again. This time when I give suggestions about a floating arm or a steel bar, their job is to internally remind themselves that it's just a thought and to say out loud, "Picture...dialogue...thought." In this way they discover that not only do I not directly cause their internal experience, but they also have an undeniable experience that what they do is more important than what I do with regards to what they experience. They can have an unbendable arm or not, depending on what they do in response to my suggestions.

If you get a client who is both highly hypnotizable and

operating out of a social mind, these types of experiences can be extra powerful.

Someone who operates out of a socialized mind means "you make me anxious" literally. They experience their emotions as directly caused by others' words and outside circumstances, and don't experience themselves as creators or co-creators of their own experience. Add to this the tendency to spontaneously drop into hypnotic states where they get absorbed into suggested experiences and have the sense that it's just happening to them. Sometimes these folks may put up a hard front of cynicism or be controlling and attempt to avoid certain situations because deep down they know how vulnerable they are.

Enter the hypnotherapist. You can of course do dramatic hypnotic work with them and help them stop smoking or let go of their migraine headache, and simultaneously reinforce their mindset when they leave thinking that you did it to them.

Another choice is to help them achieve their outcome, and have them leave with at least a bit more inner authority, a sense that they have more influence over their own internal experience than they previously thought. This last choice would be more trans-form-ational and developmental. If the client comes in with a strong belief experience of, say, other people's remarks making them anxious or shameful, then you can, as a hypnosis professional, pace and lead that "reality" like no other.

The client may have experienced others "making him or her anxious" but they won't have experienced others "making" their arm unbendable, "making" their name disappear, or "making" nonexistent dogs seem real.

If you use suggestion and hypnosis to, say, stick their hand to the wall, and they have a dramatic and real experience of you doing it to them, then that's a different league of "mind control" than the folks in their life have been able to do. When they then have the undeniable experience of being able to change the experience, by reminding themselves that it's just a suggestion, while you do the same thing, that can be mind blowing and a great pace and lead towards more self-authorship.

The astute client may protest and correctly point out that you are no longer doing the same thing, that your intent is different, and that you are implying that he or she can "resist" and therefore they are still responding to your suggestions. I have to say though that no-one has made that objection in my office. Still, an internalized authority figure's or expert's voice instructing them to "make your own decisions" can be a step (while still a socialized step) towards more self-authorship.

PRESCRIBING THE SYMPTOM LOOP

So you have done the setup, framing and imagination games. The client knows that he or she is "feeling their thinking". In other words, they think a series of "bad" thoughts and they buy into it, and it's "as real as real". They're actually in the audience and waiting for their turn to speak, but they're feeling what they would feel if they were on stage trembling with a shaky voice.

Language makes this process seem a lot more ordered and sequential than it probably is. Quite likely, what we label thoughts, images, dialogue, body sensations, emotions, movement, etc, are happening simultaneously in a way where the various components are mutually reinforcing each other in an interdependent way.

I like to evoke the feeling state through suggestion. Then I will have them feel and observe with precision at the same time. I will ask them targeted questions such as:

- Is the feeling local (in one place) or global (several places at the same time)?

- Is the feeling pressuring inwards like a contraction, outwards like an expansion, or doing both simultaneously?

- What shape or form is the feeling? Where is the boundary?

Then I will instruct the client to say the word "changing" without consciously attempting to change anything, any time there is even the slightest change.

This is somewhat paradoxical—don't try to change, but accept the experience so that it will change.

Then I may, while they feel and observe/name body sensations, have them say out loud "thought...dialogue...picture..." anytime any of those appears. As soon as the person recognizes that a thought is just a thought, a picture is just a picture, it has a tendency to break the spell. This can also be done as self-application homework.

This has a tendency to break the symptom loop. You're training them to differentiate between the body sensations and the story, and that breaks up the loop—the same as with the running in place pattern.

Again, credit to Shinzen Young for much of this. Paul Ross, who has studied personally with Shinzen, calls him the Milton Erickson of the meditation world. His CD set, *The Science of Enlightenment*, rocked my world back in 2007.

Something else you can do to make this type of symptom prescription even more effective, is to orient their attention in a way that develops and contextualizes specific skills that are incongruent with having the symptom.

Let's look at some examples:

Depression: Many who depress have a tendency to experience their depressive symptoms as something permanent and pervasive as well as taking it very personally. By orienting them to be very specific about what they are experiencing and how the experience is changing continuously, you are training them to look for, notice and ratify *change* while they do their symptom loop.

Orienting them to notice boundaries where body sensations start and stop also helps them not to make the experience pervasive. And being able to witness an experience, to observe it with precision, helps the person to no longer identify as "a depressed person", but instead be aware that they are having a transitory experience.

This also applies to pain. There is a difference between a pain signal and the amount of suffering a person experiences. You can have a lot of pain and relatively little suffering. The opposite can be just as true—you can have little pain and lots of suffering. In addition to the pain signal, which may or may not relate to actual damage, there are many other components that go into the mix of determining the total amount of suffering, such as how the person focuses on the pain signal, the meaning the person projects onto the pain, expectations of future pain, memories of past pain, fear, tensing up and other emotional factors.

Being completely present with the body sensations of pain and separating those from the imagery, thoughts and storytelling can dramatically reduce both the suffering and the pain. What I just described here is a very worthwhile lesson from Buddhist teachings of meditation.

When people do anxiety, they have a tendency to mentally be in the future. They imagine "bad" outcomes and believe in them. Often, they are playing a "what if" game where the question and imagined outcome and the body sensations mutually reinforce and amplify each other in a continuous symptom loop. There is usually some musturbating involved where they demand a certain outcome, that the feeling must go away, and/or a guarantee that others will view them a certain way before they do anything at all.

Any meditation or symptom prescription exercise that helps the client stay present, dispute their musturbating, and treat thoughts as thoughts, will likely be very useful in reducing or eliminating anxiety.

Anger is usually a more present-oriented experience. Two

excellent strategies are to identify and dispute the musturbating. Another choice is to train oneself to feel and observe
the body sensations without doing anything or engaging with
the story at all.

USING SYMPTOM WORDS

Sometimes people lean on certain words or phrases which
somehow are strongly connected to their symptom loops.

A few years ago I worked with an author who would say
"fire" when she talked about her anxiety. She would say stuff
like: "The anxiety fires off..." and "...when I fire off anxiety".
She is the only client I have ever had who used those phrases.

During the work we did I set out to liberate that fixed association. I would suggest that she could fire off new learn-
ings...that she could fire off old associations...and experience
fire in so many ways.

Remember to combine your hypnotic skills when doing
meditative approaches for the purpose of skill building and
symptom prescription. In the same way that NLP and REBT
practitioners usually pretend that the other party doesn't
exist, hypnosis professionals and meditation teachers have
a tendency to do the same. Which is unfortunate, as both
camps have a lot to teach one another. One solid counter-
example is Michael Yapko, who does a great job building a
bridge between the two worlds in his book *Mindfulness and
Hypnosis*.

Any serious student of hypnosis and its history knows
about the turf war between those who think of hypnosis as
a state and/or trait and the non-state socio-cognitive model
of hypnosis. The "state model" seems to be the most popular
among clinicians and change workers, while the socio-cognitive model has had, in general, more support among academic researchers. Persons like Milton Erickson, Dave Elman,

John Watkins, Ernest Hilgard and Herbert Spiegel are well-known and influential proponents of the state model. These guys are well-known to hypnotherapists who make their living seeing clients.

The socio-cognitive school rejects the idea of hypnosis as a state of consciousness or even hypnotic capacity as a stable trait and think that so-called hypnotic phenomena are goal-oriented behaviors by people acting out the role of being hypnotized (as they understand the role in the context defined as hypnotic). These folks think, and make a good case for, the idea that what they refer to as "hypnosis" can best be explained by the socio-cognitive factors at play in other forms of role-taking or role-engagement.

This line of thinking has been pioneered by people like Robert White, Theodore Sarbin, T.X. Barber and Nicholas Spanos. Folks like Barber and Spanos thought of hypnotizability as modifiable and showed that no hypnotic induction was needed to elicit hypnotic phenomena.

While research seems to show that most people do score a little bit better on hypnotizability testing after a hypnotic induction, some people do even better *without* a hypnotic induction. I agree when it comes to hypnotic phenomena, at least partly.

Those who do hypnotherapy will often present hypnosis as a state. After a pre-talk designed to eliminate fear and ensure cooperation, the hypnotherapist will guide the client through a so-called hypnotic induction. Here the client is most often instructed to relax and imagine various things. Some will talk about "going into trance" and/or suggest that the client go to sleep. Other hypnotherapists may use confusion or more indirect approaches. While induction methods vary, the goal is to guide the client into the alleged hypnotic state.

Unfortunately, way too many "hypnotherapists" don't test for hypnosis or use any hypnotic convincers. As a result many clients don't think they were hypnotized. This is a big problem since the frame being used is one where one has to be in a hypnotic state for change to happen. As a result, since many don't feel much different than they do when relaxed, they spend their time wondering if they are hypnotized or not instead of engaging with the suggestions.

If they don't think they were hypnotized, they spend their time doubting that any trance is going on (instead of engaging with suggestions), and have bought into a belief that says that they have to be hypnotized for the suggestions to work, then the chances for change are rather slim, although solid counter-examples do occur.

The more skilled (and courageous) hypnotherapists evoke hypnotic phenomena and convincers to demonstrate to both themselves and the client that they have been hypnotized.

One somewhat sneaky trick, popularized by people like Don Mottin and Cal Banyan, is time distortion. They will ask the client to check their watch to note what time it is before the induction begins. At the end of the session, before suggesting that they come out of hypnosis, they will give suggestions like, "You have been in hypnosis for just a few minute (priming them to think in terms of "minute" instead of "minutes")...and you will be surprised to discover just how well you have done."

Right after opening their eyes they will be asked, without looking at their watches, to estimate the time they spent in hypnosis. No-one skilled with hypnosis will ask them how *long* they think they were in hypnosis. Rather they will either ask them to estimate the time or ask them how short or brief they would estimate the time they spent in hypnosis.

The experienced professional may ask quickly with a hurried voice to indirectly suggest a brief passage of time and to stack the deck in his favor.

This borderline scam of a convincer is pretty failsafe;

when deeply relaxed or engaged in some activity people have the sense that time flies. Almost always, they will dramatically underestimate how much time has gone by. When you then have them look at the watch, they will be surprised. Then you can easily sell that as evidence that they were in fact hypnotized by reminding them of the suggestion you gave them about time, and how this means that they accepted and realized the suggestions. The good subjects will usually act on the suggestion and really underestimate the time. They will tend to underestimate the time naturally, whether or not they respond to the suggestions. Either way, you can frame it as evidence of hypnosis having taken place.

Since it's a covert test, nothing is lost if the client estimates the time more accurately. You can just say: that's interesting, and move on, since they don't know it's a test. If they are spot-on accurate when estimating the time, you can be sneaky and sell that as evidence of hypnosis too, under the guise that people who are hypnotized have proven to be better at estimating time.

While often impressive to clients, sneaky artistry like this does nothing to convince the non-state theorists of the existence of a distinct state of hypnosis.

By far the most common hypnotic phenomena used as convincers are eye catalepsy, unbendable arm and feet stuck to the floor. The suggestion is given that when the hypnotherapist reaches, say, the count of five, the more the client attempts to bend his arm, (open eyes, lift feet, etc.), the more it will remain stiff and rigid, etc.

While these types of "challenge convincers" are the most common ones, those with a more Ericksonian background may go for arm levitation or finger signals/ideomotor responses.

These phenomena are used as convincers, the premise being that experiencing these phenomena means that the client is hypnotized. Quite convincing to the client (as long as the phenomena are solid), since they haven't experienced not being able to bend their arm or open their eyes as a result of suggestion in their regular states of consciousness, it makes sense to them that they must now be in some unique state named hypnosis.

However, the non-state theorists aren't impressed by this either. Why would they be when they know that you can get unbendable arm, eye catalepsy and ideomotor signals with no hypnotic induction at all?

Consider faith healings, exorcism and voodoo rituals where healing of disease is used as evidence that God exists, where body convulsions during exorcism prove entities and higher powers at work, or where death in so-called bone-pointing rituals confirm the premises behind magical thinking.

It's easy to laugh at the "suckers" who engage in the above mentioned rituals; however they show the powers of role-engagement, imagination and ritual to evoke capacities that we may not ordinarily have access to, for better or for worse.

In the more secular western world we also use ritual and role-taking to access resources. One example would be the recent findings that in some knee operations as well as angina surgeries, dramatic outcomes have been entirely due to the placebo effect. Irving Kirsch demonstrates convincingly in his book, *The Emperor's New Drugs*, that the whole chemical imbalance theory of depression is bunk and that the "patients" have been "treated" through the power of suggestion. Rituals do reach the modern mind far better when white coats, medical doctors, drugs, theories of chemical imbalances and dramatic surgeries rule the show. While the rituals used to reach the more mythic mind may seem silly from a modern perspective, the same socio-cognitive factors seem to be at play. They are both acting out the role of a sick person, as they understand the role, in a context defined as religious healing or medical treatment as defined by proper authority within that cultural context.

When speaking about role-taking or role-engagement, it's important to point out that I'm not talking about merely faking or pretending. When I engage and play with my daughter, Rikke, I'm not faking anything. I'm as authentic and loving as my being allows. At the same time the historical period that Rikke and I live in—and the culture and social system we are part of—influence how we act out of the roles of father and daughter. It's simultaneously authentic and made up.

The participants on reality shows such as *The Bachelorette* do fall in love, *and* fall in love in alignment with their understanding of their role as part of a reality show. It's authentic and socially constructed at the same time.

Both the soldiers who tortured at Abu Graibh, and the participants in Philip Zimbardo's infamous prison experiment acted out their horrific torture and bullying in alignment with how they understood their roles as soldiers and prison guards as defined by their superiors.

The very un-sexy claim of the socio-cognitive theorists is that so-called hypnotic behaviors are much more mundane than commonly assumed. It can be explained by the same socio-cognitive factors that explain the behaviors of voodoo participants, reality show contestants and fanatical soccer fans during matches. How can this view of hypnosis be useful?

BRAIN SURGERY WITHOUT KNIVES

In any field, the metaphors that we operate out of will influence not only how we view things but what we are able to see. Western medicine strongly operates out of the "human body as machine" metaphor. This metaphor influences what medical professionals look for and the information they find, which further reinforces the metaphor and its underlying assumptions.

Drugs and surgery fit within the metaphor of the body as a machine. I'm not knocking it—medicine is doing a lot of good and has contributed enormously to human well-being. At the same time, consciousness, internal conflicts, thoughts and emotions don't easily find a home within that metaphor. Neither do the effects of culture and relationships. To explore these domains, other metaphors will be more useful.

Various schools of psychotherapy, coaching and hypnosis have various metaphors and frameworks. They encourage us to look for information that fits and discard or not even notice information that doesn't fit. All ways of understanding are partial and simultaneously ways of *not* understanding.

Take heart disease as an example. Medical students are likely to know quite a bit about the dangers of smoking, a bad diet and lack of exercise as it fits the machine metaphor. They are less likely to be aware of the studies that show how anger, hostility and loneliness are risk factors. The chances of them having heard about the Roseto story are probably rather slim.

During the '50s and '60s the city of Roseto, Pennsylvania

in the USA, became well known for having very low rates of heart disease, stroke and a host of other diseases compared to its neighboring cities. Scientists were intrigued by this fact and set out to figure out what was going on. The people that lived there mostly originated from Roseto, Italy. The researchers suspected a genetic answer, but discovered that people from Roseto who lived in other cities didn't seem to have the same protection from some diseases as those who lived in Roseto. Shockingly, the folks in Roseto did not have a particularly healthy diet, nor were they big on exercise. Many were, in fact, overweight.

After a while the scientists concluded that the social life, rituals and culture in Roseto had to play a big part. The culture was very social and family-oriented, had plenty of rituals to make sure that everyone felt included and no-one was left out. Even though some were financially better off than others, they lived modest lives.

What happened next strengthened the scientists' position. Over time, as the kids went to college and came home and changed the culture into one that was more individualistic and materialistic, the rate of heart disease and stroke reached the levels of its neighboring cities.

Being able to look at and take into account factors such as nutrition, smoking, psychology, culture and social factors simultaneously when dealing with, say, heart disease, seems to require the ability to be able to utilize several metaphors and frameworks without being married to any of them as the truth with a capital T.

Let's take a look at two different scenarios, one defined as hypnotic and the other as medical, and see what they have in common from a non-state perspective.

I sometimes have interesting exchanges of perspectives with a clinical hypnotist by the name of Barry Thain. Barry often conceptualizes hypnosis as brain surgery without knives. He thinks of hypnosis as a sleep-like state of mind and as something that he does *to* the other person. Like most of those who think of hypnosis as a state, he also thinks that it's something that some brains have the "neurological architecture" for and others don't. Where Barry seems somewhat different than most state theorists is that most view hypnosis as guided self-hypnosis instead of a "do-to" process. Accepting the metaphor of "brain surgery without knives" will incline a person to interpret information in alignment with that metaphor.

Barry once showed me a very interesting short clip. Even more interesting to me was how he made sense out of it.

In the clip, Barry meets a client (Barry calls them patients and thinks of what he's doing as a treatment) at the door and he blindfolds himself after leading her to the hypnosis chair. The woman has been to his office at least once before, and I believe this is session number two. He touches her hands slightly and places them on her lap. He is blindfolded and can't *see* her hands, but his head is positioned in such way that his covered-up eyes are directed towards them. They exchange no words.

Then, seemingly much to the surprise of the woman, her arms start moving involuntarily and these movements continue for quite a while. If I remember correctly, the hands lock together in the end.

It's a very cool demo, one that does not find a home within most people's framework, which may persuade many to project either some entity/supernatural force at work, mind control and/or the woman being in a distinct hypnotic state where Barry is in direct Svengali-like control of her mind.

Barry believes she is in a hypnotic state. He further believes that he is *causing* the hypnosis as well as directing her movements with his mind.

I haven't interviewed the woman, but her facial expressions, to me, show confusion and surprise. It's clear that she does not think that she is moving her own hands. Both believe that Barry is causing it with his mind. Her contribution is to show up and to have the necessary "neurological architecture".

The reason Barry showed me the clip was that I was pointing out the many outdated and flawed premises of the "power hypnotists" on a public forum he was hosting.

I was doing my best to alert the rest of the audience to the fact that the more scientifically oriented members of our profession have moved to a "do with" orientation and left fantasies of mind control behind.

The power hypnotists countered that they were doing *real* hypnosis. When I asked for proof that they could do anything that those of us practicing "unreal hypnosis" couldn't do, Barry stepped up with his clip. In his mind, that clip shows a distinct hypnotic state and him directly causing the hypnotic state as well as directing her arm movements with his mind.

Her arms moving like that, in a non-volitional way, were evidence to Barry of her being in a distinct hypnotic state.

Barry then challenged me to replicate what he did.

While I don't think the socio-cognitive angle offers a complete explanation, it does offer quite a bit with regards to explain what happened, and just as important, what did not happen.

1. First of all, no distinct physiological state has been found that can support the idea of a hypnotic trance state exclusive to the hypnosis lab or hypnotherapist's office.

2. The context is defined as a hypnotic one where both Barry and the client are in agreement as to what their roles are.

111

Barry's job is to direct her experience—he is the hypnotist. Her role is to respond, and to do so in a way that she
experiences as non-volitional.

If she had deliberately lifted her hands and experienced herself as doing so voluntarily, it would not have qualified as
a hypnotic response. On the other hand, the experience of
having her hands lifting by themselves while subjectively experiencing it as non-volitional and happening in response to
the hypnotist's suggestions, does qualify.

A socio-cognitive model credits the hypnotic subject as
an active participant in the process—a process where her expectations, beliefs, motives, imaginative capacities (fantasy
proneness, absorption) combined with how she understands
her role, determine how she enacts her role as a hypnotic
subject.

In the previous session she had experienced the hypnotic
phenomena of her hands being stuck together, that was experienced as non-volitional and was her reference of what it
was like to be hypnotized.

When Barry leads her into the office, touches her hands
and organizes them on her lap (while she is sitting), then
points his head towards her hands (while he is blindfolded),
he is offering a nonverbal suggestion that something is going
to happen to her hands. Her past reference for being hypnotized also involved her hands.

At first she is clearly confused, which isn't so strange considering how the blindfolded hypnotist is pointing his head
towards her hands and not saying a word. How is she to act,
and how does she make sense out of the situation?

Well, the non-verbal suggestion is that something is supposed to happen to her hands—she has a reference for that

in her previous session—and the context is defined as a hypnotic one. In other words, her job is to have her hands move, experience it as non-volitional, and credit Barry as the one who is doing it to her. There are a few contexts where the combination of verbal and non-verbal suggestion, non-volitional responses and the belief that someone else is causing the responses are not labeled hypnosis nor attributed to a hypnotic state.

Consider faith healings and religious ceremonies. Here people may experience instant pain relief, healing of disease, fainting and convulsions. The various responses are non-volitional and happen as part of a ritual where the subjects are given suggestions by someone credited with special powers of expertise. The credit goes to the alleged God and/or the priest.

Since the participants haven't experienced—or perhaps haven't defined—these experiences elsewhere, they are likely to conclude that what they experienced is evidence that God exists or that the expert has special powers and caused their experience.

I remember watching, in amusement, a religious nut, Benny Hinn, who ran around on a platform screaming *"Fire!"* and the disciples fell to the floor. Some of them merely complied and deliberately lay down. Others were responding to the suggestion in a non-volitional way.

The martial artist George Dillman is famous for his pressure point knockouts and, believe it or not, *no-touch* knockouts. He will knock out students and carefully picked seminar participants without touching them. In George's case this is allegedly proof of the existence of chi power and George's masterful ability to direct it.

A TV team exposed the flawed premises behind the no-touch knockouts. First they filmed George knocking out his students using both pressure point and no-touch versions. Medical personnel verified, through their equipment, that the students weren't faking their responses.

Then poor old George was dragged to a mixed martial arts gym. These guys are kickboxing and grappling. The sparring is rough, and the training is hardcore.

The same thing happened that would have happened if the religious nut who screamed *"Fire!"* had done so at an atheist's convention. No-one would have fallen to the floor although some might have run towards the fire exit.

None of the mixed martial artists were affected by George's techniques at all...zero effect.

I declined Barry's challenge based on this line of reasoning, and I pointed out that people like George Dillman and leaders of religious and spiritual ceremonies got non-volitional responses to nonverbal and verbal suggestion in alignment with the participants' roles, as they understood the role in that context. Therefore Barry had neither demonstrated some distinct hypnotic state, nor that he could accomplish direct mind control.

In the spirit of friendly combat I issued the following challenge to Barry and the self-defined "real hypnotists". I proposed that he first would have to actually demonstrate mind control. Furthermore I proposed that he hit the streets and do something that grabs people's attention—perhaps just sitting across from people on a train with a blindfold on (you could of course skip the blindfold). Then use mind control and get the same type of outcome that he got in his office. No verbal or non-verbal suggestions, and no-one could know that he was a hypnotist. He declined the challenge.

Too many hypnotists and hypnotherapists seem blind to the situational, contextual and relationship factors that go into the mix during hypnotic experiments and interventions.

One example of this is how many people made sense of Derren Brown's show, *The Assassin*.

During the show Brown scans for hypnotic talent, and after a thorough selection process, he selects the most highly hypnotizable person among the participants. Brown then spends some time training the participant and gives hypnotic suggestions, plus amnesia for those suggestions, designed to create an assassin. The hypnotically trained Manchurian candidate then, after a cue, rises and carries out the post-hypnotic suggestion and proceeds to shoot a well-known person at a theater.

As you probably guessed (and who wouldn't) the gun wasn't loaded.

Still many consider Derren's stunt as evidence that you can create a Manchurian candidate using hypnosis. It's one thing for people without any relevant knowledge and training to reach such a conclusion. It's something else when alleged professionals do so.

Anyone with some appreciation of context will realize that Derren Brown did *not* prove that you can create a Manchurian candidate using hypnosis.

Any participant with modest abilities in reality testing, knows that the BBC (or whoever produced it) and Derren Brown would *never* in a million years risk the consequences of one of their TV show participants actually shooting someone on TV with a loaded gun they had given him after giving instruction to kill during hypnosis.

In the back of his mind the "assassin" knows that the gun isn't loaded and that he is a participant in a TV show where a famous mentalist is going to have him do something which isn't quite what it seems.

You can be sure that Brown is scanning for someone awake enough to understand his role in addition to high hypnotic capacity.

Let's assume that none of what I just wrote is true. Let's imagine that both Brown and the TV production company and their lawyers where crazy enough to hypnotically train someone to kill someone and then hand him a loaded gun. Let's also assume that the participants are as nuts as they are and think it's for real.

It still wouldn't prove much. A bloodthirsty psychopath with a desire to kill may carry out the assignment, blame the hypnosis, and likely get off the hook. Then he could sue Brown, or the company responsible for the setup, for everything they've got—killing someone on TV, being famous, getting off in the legal system, and being so well compensated that he wouldn't have to work another day in his entire life.

Not too bad a deal for a bloodthirsty psychopath, whether hypnotized or not.

THE NORWEGIAN NURSE RATCHED

I will never forget the night at the hospital when my wife, Marit, gave birth to our daughter Rikke. Neither will I forget the Norwegian version of Nurse Ratched who visited us the next day. This woman, and way too many like her, contribute to massive amounts of symptoms and suffering during their "supportive" talks with new mothers and other patients. You could call it the dark side of suggestion and hypnosis. It's not only dark in terms of unnecessary and therefore unethical suffering—it's doubly dark in that she has no clue about what she is doing due to her having no training in the art of hypnosis. It gets worse; the patients and their families are just as clueless. In general, due to the current establishment metaphors and framework for understanding symptoms, they have little, if any, appreciation of how they and the nurse are co-creators of much of the unnecessary suffering that awaits them.

Nurse Ratched came into our room to have a well-intended supportive and informative talk with the new mother. This is common procedure. So far, so good.

The nurse opened the show by introducing herself and the informative/supportive frame.

She then offered some truism and general pacing statements such as, "This is a new situation for the both of you... life will change in many ways...you're probably wondering

117

what life will be like...you both have your own ideas, questions and concerns..."

The truisms and general statements are so vague that they pretty much ensure agreement. In both sales and hypnosis, this is often used to establish a "yes set" where the person goes into an agreeable mode that makes it more likely that they will continue agreeing.

After a while she starts talking about mood swings, anxiety and feelings of inadequacy and anger. First she is somewhat general and vague, *then* she directly states that 80% of new mothers are out in the hallway after a couple of days, weeping and breaking down, and how important it is to let that happen. She proceeds to tell Marit that she *will* have the various reactions, that she *will* be anxious and angry.

Incredibly, she then offers a bunch of post-hypnotic suggestions where she links the various feelings to cues in Marit's environment. One of them was especially memorable: "You may be sitting on the couch relaxing and everything seems fine...and then your mother-in-law says something...and you just explode in anger...it just happens, and you can't help it."

At this point I had had enough, so I started to pick her whole presentation apart. I did so by challenging her absolutism and certainty by asking questions such as, "Does *everybody* get anxious? Can you be certain that she will experience this? Does she really have no choice and can't help what she feels? Would it be OK if she skipped the suggested misery and felt good?"

Reluctantly, very reluctantly, she had to admit that Marit didn't have to expect or experience what she was suggesting, and that quite a few people did not. And yes, it was OK to be happy.

Let's look at this.

Most new mothers (and old) will be operating at least partly from a socialized mind. They are likely to have internalized the common establishment assumptions regarding health, what it means to be a mother, the body-as-machine metaphor, etc. Authority is an internalized value/principle and role which comes from outside herself. The socialized mind is therefore likely to accept the nurse as an expert and authority due to her position.

The socialized mother will unconsciously attempt to adjust her own behavior in accordance with how the new mother role is defined by the nurse/expert.

She is therefore likely to internalize and act out of the expectations she is picking up from the nurse. Of course the fatigue and uncertainty contribute to the new mother being extra vulnerable and reliant on the experts to define how she is supposed to act and feel.

Our Nurse Ratched is good at establishing a yes set through her truisms and pacing statements. This way rapport, trust and responsiveness are increased.

When the nurse directly states that 80% of new mothers are out in the hallway breaking down and weeping after a couple of days, she is a danger to her patients. Many of the mothers—around 80%—internalize that expectation and respond by acting out their role as defined by the nurse.

Research in social psychology has demonstrated the power of social proof. People have a tendency—especially when they are insecure and vulnerable—to do what most others seem to do. One common example of social proof is how an empty restaurant has a tendency to scare customers away and how a visibly popular restaurant draws new customers to it. Many restaurant/bar owners have discovered that customers leave more tips if they see a tip bucket with quite a bit of

119

money in it, suggesting that most people tip here.

I asked the nurse if telling the mothers during her informational talks about 80% of them breaking down in the hallway was common procedure. She said yes.

In her mind she was just offering accurate information. She had no awareness whatsoever that she was an important co-creator of the subsequent breakdowns through her role combined with suggestion.

Neither did she have any sense that her direct suggestions were influential in others internalizing her expectations and acting them out. The nurse herself operated out of a socialized mind. It was clear she had internalized the norms, assumptions and expectations of her profession and was behaving according to protocol. She was happy to impose the standard patient role on her patients with the conviction that she knew best. The idea of asking questions and respecting the patient as a unique human being with choices about how to respond did not seem to be on her radar screen.

I don't know how many people would have had a "breakdown" without Nurse Ratched's contribution, but it would not have been 80%. While the nurse was giving her suggestions the patients were "thinking with" those suggestions.

It may or may not be accurate to label an interaction like this hypnosis. The reason I am tempted to do so is because hypnotic experience and behavior is both purposeful and non-volitional. When the mothers have their breakdowns and burst out at their mothers-in-law, just as suggested, they experience it as non-volitional—it just happens to them. Unlike Barry the "brain surgeon" the nurse does not think that she is causing their symptoms. Just like with Barry's patient and George's knockout victims, the mothers don't view themselves as playing a part in creating their own responses.

One big difference is that the hypnotized patient and the knockout victims at least know in which context it happened;

the mothers are not likely to connect any of the ensuing symptoms to the informative talks. They will interpret the symptoms in alignment with their deeper assumptions and beliefs. Most will blame hormones and external factors, others' (and babies') demands combined perhaps with deprivation of sleep. These factors may of course all play a part in their experience, but the contextual, expectation and suggestion factors will seldom be thought of, as they don't have much of a place in most folks' framework. The nurse will likely interpret it along the same lines and become even more convinced and congruent when delivering her informational talks.

I voiced my concerns and offered some ideas for how she could simultaneously deliver her information and not only reduce the breakdowns and symptoms, but also help the mothers connect better to their resources during her talk. She was somewhat hurried and politely listened, but I don't think I reached her.

Her role is to be an expert and to act responsibly by following protocol. If she is to change how she does things, then doctors with proper authority will have to teach and instruct her. Furthermore, experts who are embedded in the implicit assumptions of their field are likely to think that if there was any significant truth to an idea proposed by an outsider, then they would already be doing it. After all, they are experts.

The ability to step back from the assumptions of one's field, to question authority, and to take responsibility for self-defining one's role are the capacities of a more self-authoring mind. Unfortunately, most adults are not yet self-authoring.

A self-authoring, or even self-transforming mind, would be way less likely to develop the symptoms suggested by the nurse. To the self-authoring mind, authority lies in the self, and she designs her own role and standards for motherhood.

For the more self-transforming mind, authority is more

context-dependent and fluid. While this person will be more open to feedback and others' perspectives and use those to transform her own inner system, she is not prone to have other people push roles or beliefs down her throat. The self-authored and self-transforming mind won't be impressed by titles or the idea of an authority figure that wants to define their experience for them.

For the earliest (adult) meaning-making system, the self-sovereign mind, authority is external and found in rules, regulations and people who have power over them.

As far as I can tell there is no link between these types of mind systems and hypnotic capacity.

I'd like you to consider something else. The involuntary arm movements Barry's client demonstrated fit the hypnotherapeutic context. If he had guided her into hypnosis and then directly suggested that she would have depressive symptoms, get really anxious and begin to blow up at her mother-in-law, it wouldn't make much sense for her to accept those suggestions. You can't know for sure, she may have underlying self-destructive motives, but accepting those suggestions wouldn't fit the context.

Likewise, had Nurse Ratched suggested that her new mother's arms would begin to move involuntarily, or asked about the color of the (hallucinated) dog sitting next to them, then they would most assuredly pop out of their agreeable mode and conclude that she was more than a little nuts.

The point is this: When using the art of suggestion, you've got to take role, relationship and contextual factors into account. You've got to create a context where responding to the suggestions make sense. And you've got to appreciate the client as an active meaning-maker. Even when deeply hypnotized, the client is not a blank slate. Those who think so are usually people who have fallen for the Cartesian catastrophe, namely reducing all thinking and meaning-making to consciousness. This implies that we know what we think (all of it), and that non-conscious thought doesn't exist.

Too many hypnotherapy instructors teach that the conscious mind is the thinking mind and that the unconscious mind just feels, and that if you can bypass the conscious mind then you can program in whatever you want. Modern cognitive science shows that it's time for most hypnotherapists to update their frameworks.

Much of our thinking and meaning-making is indeed non-conscious. The client's expectations, beliefs, implicit assumptions and unconscious motives influence how they make sense out of suggestions. Their form of mind, whether self-sovereign, socialized, self-authoring or self-transforming, matters a lot. It matters not in terms of hypnotizability, but it influences how they view responsibility, their ability for perspective-taking, relationship to authority and the dichotomies that shape what is self and what is other.

Then we have the client's cognitive skill directly related to hypnotizability: Skills of vivid imagery and absorption, to be able to imagine something "as real as real"—capacity for dissociation and responding to suggestion in either a way that truly is non-volitional or interpreted as non-volitional and the ability to go into an altered state of consciousness.

Finally, consider how the suggestion Marit was given with the regards to her mother-in-law. How the patient feels about and relates to her mother-in-law will matter in terms of if/how she makes sense of that suggestion.

Before we leave that topic, know that there are some great counter-examples to Nurse Ratched in the medical world. One medical doctor by the name of Lewis Walker has integrated NLP and hypnotic skills into his medical practice for over two decades. When he prescribes medication and has to mention potential side effects, he will describe them while using an upward inflection into his voice tone. This has a tendency to trigger doubt in the listener. He also uses suggestion to link experiencing side effects with the client, using it as evidence that the meds are working and that they are moving towards health. Here, embedded commands, implication, anchoring and suggestion artistry is used for multi-level communication. He is simultaneously offering information while minimizing symptoms and connecting experiencing symptoms to resourceful states and perspectives. These are also skills that Richard Bandler has emphasized while teaching nurses and doctors.

While the socio-cognitive angle offers a lot, it comes up short. Let's push it as far as we can, as we go back to using hypnotic phenomena and then complement it with the benefits of a state-/trait-based way of viewing hypnosis.

THE HAND STICK

A few years ago a good friend and competent hypnotist by the name of James Tripp released a product called *Hypnosis Without Trance*. James rejects the idea that you need to induce a trance state to evoke hypnotic phenomena. Like many before him he has discovered that neither the concept of trance nor the ritualistic induction of an alleged hypnotic state is necessary to evoke various hypnotic phenomena.

James has some intriguing ideas and very pragmatic ways of getting hypnotic phenomena that removes the bullshit and hugga-bugga factors from hypnosis.

The main reason for mentioning James here is that I have had a lot of use for his format for both the hand stick and name amnesia.

I have also developed some functional applications of these for change work that I would like to share with you.

You can frame any of these as an imagination game, the opportunity for the client to learn something interesting about how his mind works, or of course you can ask him if he would like to experience some hypnotic phenomena.

James has done quite a bit of street hypnosis and mentalism. Instead of the mind control/submission and dominance games that most street and stage hypnotists tend to play, James both views and frames it as a more interactive experience where the subject plays a part, and where the both of them co-create a cool experience. This is more in alignment with my personal preferences. While I have been more

125

than willing to learn from street and stage performers, I have never liked the power hypnotist/mind control frames that almost all of them operate out of.

While the format that follows isn't word for word identical with James's, it's essentially the same and full credit goes to James.

1. My preference is to have them put their palm pressing slightly into the wall. This way the physiology supports the suggested phenomena. Part of artistry is to stack all the decks in your favor.

2. Focus Attention: Instruct the subject to find a spot on the back of their hand to focus on. You may say something like, "As you focus all your attention on that spot...the sound of my voice...and other sounds you may become aware of...can all become a part of you really *focus* all your *attention on* that spot." Make sure that you utilize any distracting sounds or whatever happens.

3. Imaginative Absorption: Here you want them to imagine the hand being glued or stuck to the wall to the point where it's experienced "as real as real".

You may say something like, "And as you continue to focus on that spot...you can be aware of the back of your hand (pace)...see the nail of your little finger (pace)...see your thumb (pace)...you can *feel that palm* ("that" palm primes dissociation) *press* (embedded command) against the wall... and as you keep seeing *that* hand...while you're listening to the sound of my voice...you can *feel your fingers* press into the wall...only as quickly as you begin to *imagine that hand is stuck* to the wall *now*...imagine glue on that hand *sticking* and locking that hand to the wall...to the point where...you can *feel it stuck...now.*"

Needless to say, you want to calibrate the person's

responses and utilize them. And whenever you see any involuntary response, however slight, make sure to say something like "that's right" to amplify it. Also utilize any response by using "the more you X the more you can experience Y" so that you pace and lead towards the stuck hand.

4. Soft Test: Here you want to do a soft test. Say something like this: "And as you *feel that hand is stuck...now...*which part of that hand feels the most stuck...your palm or your fingers?"

Here we have a classic double bind. The question presupposes that the hand is stuck, the question is: which part is *most* stuck? This also presupposes that both palm and fingers are stuck.

5. Amplify Response: Let's say the person says that their palm is most stuck. Now you want to use that stuck palm to develop more stuck fingers: "*That's right*...and notice how really becoming aware of how *that* palm is stuck... makes those fingers even more stuck...to the point where that hand is stuck to the wall."

Before getting to know James I was not in the habit of asking clients to verbalize their responses during the process of eliciting phenomena. But verbalizing can be useful because the person may tell you that the hand isn't stuck, but instead report some other sensation in their hand. Once you know about it, you can utilize it.

Most people will be able to get absorbed into this. In the rare event that they don't, and claim that nothing is happening with either palm or fingers, you can ask them what's happening internally. Sometimes they have misunderstood something or are, for some reason, not engaging. Others don't have the skill at imagery and absorption necessary. You may, depending on the client's non-verbal and verbal responses, adjust your approach or go ahead and do something else. If the client doesn't seem able to do imagery and absorption, that's useful to know.

6. Hard Test: Now, assuming that calibration tells you so, it's time to suggest the full-blown hand stick. I usually say something like this: "When I touch you on the shoulder you're going to find that that hand is so stuck to the wall... that the more you try to remove it...the more it sticks. Then I touch their shoulder."

7. HAVE THEM RATIFY EXPERIENCE.

Say something to the effect of, "What's that like? The harder you try to remove it...the more it sticks." If you have solid phenomena going you will see the amusement, surprise, wonder, shock or even fear in their face. The most common verbalization is some variant of "this is weird", "holy shit", "what the fuck", or "It's stuck!!" Having them verbalize reduces the chances of the person later thinking and saying that they could have removed their hand if they really wanted to.

Some will have an undeniable mind-blowing experience of not being able to remove their hand despite consciously attempting to do so. It really fries their circuits when they experience that the more they try the more stuck the hand becomes. Some may have a partial both/and experience where they simultaneously experience it as stuck and also know it's an illusion. Others may remove it partially or completely after some struggle. A few will be completely absorbed into the experience of the hand being stuck, but pop out of the experience as soon as the hard test comes and instantly remove it.

And yes, some will just roll their eyes and remove their hand with a smirk on their face, and you will likely want to strangle the smug prick. Needless to say, you haven't calibrated well. The most amusing ones are the very few who roll their eyes and/or give you a smug smile and then to their own surprise discover that they can't remove their hand.

8. Terminate. Just tell them that when you touch them on the shoulder the hand will unstick.

APPLICATIONS

All the responses can be utilized to help people develop both insights and choice regarding their symptom loops.

I usually use the frame mentioned earlier, that I borrowed from Shinzen Young. Specifically, a symptom is thoughts, body sensations and emotions plus resistance.

One thing that I love about the hand stick is that the client is given the opportunity to discover how the way they deliberately use their imagination and capacity for absorption directly creates their experience in a step-by-step way.

The hypnotic element is the experience of non-volition as their hand is sticking.

Clients experience their symptoms—especially their feelings—as involuntary, and after a convincing hand stick many are able to discover that even if the feelings are *experienced* as involuntary, there is a cognitive imaginable process that leads to the feelings. This process can be hijacked, changed and altered.

If the hand stick is convincing, the client also discovers that once absorbed into an "as real as real" experience, the attempt to resist or "make it stop" can in fact contribute to the experience getting stronger.

Depressed Clients

Quite a few of my formerly depressed clients have discovered both the structure of their depressing, as well as how to alter it, through the hand stick.

Often depression can be a "frog soup" type phenomenon —a state they get themselves into so slowly that it's below their ability to notice until they find themselves "stuck in the mud". Once stuck, their excessive rumination and attempts to control their thinking contributes to them getting even more stuck.

Some clients have resolved their depressing indirectly through the hand stick in a metaphorical way.

Just like with the book and balloon, and unbendable arm games, you can guide them through the hand stick and have them notice what happens when they relax during the perceived stuckness and remind themselves that their thoughts, imagery and body sensations are just that and nothing more.

Anxious Clients

Anxious clients often play "what if" games of things going badly and then get absorbed into the resulting imagery and experience some potential screw up "as real as real". The hand stick, you can point out, is a "what if" game. You're playing a "what if that hand were stuck" game and get so into it that it's experienced as non-volitional and real. It's often very useful when the client discovers that he can both play the game as well as not play it as a result of how he attends to his own experience.

Don't underestimate the potential effect of using a hand stick as a metaphor. Some may have a lot of resistance to the idea that they can deliberately change their symptom.

Often this is related to past attempts to solve it through willpower and rumination. In cases like this you can often sidestep the resistance by using the hand stick first and then help them to discover the structural similarity of the hypnotic loop and the symptom loop. Some make the connection unconsciously and spontaneously, others do it through having it pointed out and/or by symptom prescription.

Let's look at how the various responses to the hand stick can be used as resources when prescribing the symptom loop.

A. Those who become completely absorbed into the hand stick can be helped to realize that not only are they the ones who create the experience, but they can also deliberately create different experiences in the problem context.

Helping them deliberately create "as real as real" hand stick and then un-create it by reminding themselves that it's "just a suggestion" can be applied to deliberately creating the symptom in the same way.

B. Those who have a partial experience where it's real and not real at the same time can be helped by discovering that this experience can be a resource when applied to the symptom loop. I say something like, "...as you experience X how it can seem real and illusory at the same time... and notice how that both/and perspective...changes your experience...is altered."

C. Those who get absorbed but "pull out" during the hard test challenge can be helped by realizing that they can "pull out" of any experience by shifting their attention, even if it's an experience that seems very real. Once again your skills in suggestion artistry are essential in helping them connect that resource to various cues and contexts.

D. Even those who completely fail the hand stick demonstrate a valuable resource—the ability to be completely unaffected by both others' suggestions and their own internal imagery. That ability can be evoked in both indirect and direct ways.

PHENOMENA FIRST—HYPNOSIS LATER

Almost without exception, those who use hypnotic phenomena do it after a hypnotic induction ritual to convince themselves and their clients that the client is in a hypnotic state.

I more often reverse this sequence. I elicit one or more hypnotic phenomena first using suggestion. Then I may do a more formal hypnotic process with the intent of helping clients re-organize and re-associate their internal world in some context. I tell them that they can just let things happen and/ or engage like they did with the phenomena. This way they don't spend their time wondering whether they are in trance or not. Quite often I don't even call it hypnosis, but just refer to it as an eyes-closed process. It's often easier for people to make effective changes when they no longer believe that they have to reach some special hypnotic state to do so. Paradoxically, this often helps people experience altered states of consciousness.

APPLICATIONS

If you get a solid hand stick going you can use that to lend credibility to direct suggestions. So, as they verbally and non-verbally confirm the hand stick you may say, "And in the same way that *that* hand is stuck...when you go into sales meetings...you are focused and present...you want to succeed...and you no longer believe that you must...only that you can."

After a little while you can end it by suggesting that in a few seconds the hand will unstick only as quickly as the other suggestion sticks even deeper into their unconscious.

Be aware though that the acceptance of one suggestion or phenomenon is never a guarantee that they will engage with some other suggestion.

However, if you're going to use some direct suggestions it does help you to link the suggestions to other suggested experience which is "as real as real"—since X is happening, Y will happen as well.

An Interesting Tinnitus Application

A couple of years ago I saw a client for tinnitus. Two things seemed clear during the first session. She seemed to have very little ability to notice any patterns when it came to relationships between her own thinking and behaving and her feelings.

My questions aimed at getting her to notice patterns, think about her own thinking and self-reflect were met with confusion. She also had a lot of trouble with naming her own emotions with any more subtlety than "bad", "mad", "sick" and "good".

Furthermore, her thinking style was black and white with very little nuance. In other words she was not psychologically oriented. These were all hints that she operated out of a self-sovereign mind. This meaning-making system is previous to the socialized mind.

These folks can be tough to work with and may reject any approach that seems too psychological. The black and white thinking style and lack of perspective-taking makes their world very concrete and obvious. They know what's up and

see things as they are, and they may be extra quick in labeling you as stupid, evil or nuts if you don't see eye to eye with
them. This isn't unique to the self-sovereign mind; it's just
harder for them not to do so.

To be able to help people with psychosomatic issues it's
exactly the ability to notice patterns, utilize symptoms as a
form of communication, use focused attention and the ability
to get absorbed into imagery that matters. Some of these resources belong to the agent of change and others to the client.

While she was clearly limited when it came to self-reflection and perspective-taking, she had the capabilities for absorption, dissociation and suggestibility in spades.

For those with decent hypnotic capacity, the hypnotic
doorway can often be a good way to reach them—that and behavioral interventions. These folks may be open to hypnosis
and resistant to psychology.

Her tinnitus was severe, constant and only fluctuated minimally. She suggested it to be between 7–8 on a 1–10 scale.

Her hypnotic abilities were very impressive. We started
off with a hand stick and it was "as real as real". I further suggested that she close her eyes...go into the deepest hypnotic
state...and enter the control room in her mind.

Once there, I suggested that there was a volume control
there that represented the volume of the ringing in her ears.

It didn't take long for her to find it. She reported that the
control knob was presently set at a 7 on the scale. I should
also point out that she didn't just imagine the scale, she hallucinated it, and it was as real to her as the ringing in her ears.

First I suggested that by increasing the volume control to
7 ½, the ringing would increase, and it did.

We practiced alternating between increasing it and re-
turning it to the baseline. The contrast of her expressions

illustrated the difference between increase and decrease in suffering.

It's usually easier, when doing hypnotic symptom prescription, to begin with actually slightly *increasing* the suffering instead of attempting to go directly for symptom relief.

After a while of playing with the scale we were able to get it down to zero, and the tinnitus vanished. She broke out in tears of joy and relief. I gave her some post-hypnotic suggestions, suggesting that her unconscious could organize things in such a way that those very same cues for tinnitus in her life could now instead be reminders for her unconscious to keep the volume control at a zero on the scale.

She was ecstatic when she left my office. However, the change held up for less than a day, and when she came back for her next session three days later, the tinnitus was back at a 7.

We did another session where we eased more slowly into it. I can't quite remember what else we did, but the results were once again just as dramatic.

We scheduled a third appointment, but she called in sick. I don't think she really was, and like last time, her symptoms were back.

My hunch is that she was as depressed and discouraged— even more so—when it came back as she was ecstatic when it left.

She never did come back, and I'm as convinced as I can be that she still has her tinnitus. I think that she thinks that hypnosis was an "it" that worked for a little, but then the "it" stopped working. The highly hypnotizable can often be easy come easy go. They may have dramatic initial results due to their ability to make real new realities, but these new realities are often vulnerable and transitory. Yes, sometimes you can just suggest symptoms away and get permanent results. It's especially tempting to do so with the highly hypnotizable since the results can be so dramatic. Combine high hypno-tizability with a self-sovereign mind, where the future is the now that hasn't happened yet, and you sometimes need to "make something happen fast" that will last.

Regression work can be an excellent choice.

Some reassociation of experience using anchors can work wonders. The agent of change will usually have to have a rather directive role. With this client, even though she was able to turn her tinnitus up and down, she did not seem to get the insight that she had choice; rather "it" worked and then "it" no longer worked, and she gave up.

There may of course be other factors at work here that are more important than those I mentioned.

Cases like this point out one flaw in the socio-cognitive perspective around hypnosis. The highly hypnotizable can do a lot of stuff (like this client) that those with low capacity just can't do. This suggests a more trait and/or state explanation.

Name Amnesia

James Tripp's format for eliciting name amnesia is rather similar to the hand stick and also something I have been able to utilize in creative ways. I have mostly used it as a metaphor and as a tool to help clients loosen stuck perspectives, beliefs and identity statements.

First I will give you the pattern and then an example from my private practice.

1. Frame the experience. Use the "opportunity to learn something" frame or co-create a frame based upon what your client has given you.

2. Prime the pump: Talk about common occurrences of for-getting (forgetting someone's name that you just met, los-ing your train of thought in a conversation, etc.). Slightly mark out words like *forget* and *name*. Anchor by doing

the same visual gesture every time you give an example of forgetting. I usually mention two or three examples.

3. Ask: "But you do remember your own name?" Use a doubting voice tone.

In rare instances their name will be gone. In most good subjects you will see them hesitate just a little before they say their name.

4. Ask: As you remember your name...where is it? (You want them to point to where the name is located. Later you're going to have them change *where* they locate the name spatially.)

5. Have them imagine that you're grabbing hold of their name...and that it's moving away...beyond the building...the city limits...all the way...until it's *gone*. Quickly suggest that as they look at you, it's gone.

6. Test: "What's it like as you try and find your name and it's *gone*."

As long as you keep their eyes fixated on you they will have difficulty accessing their name which is at the location you spatially put it. This pattern is a changing location sub-modality pattern combined with suggested imagery. It's another step-by-step procedure where you have the opportunity to calibrate whether the client is engaging with the process and getting absorbed into the suggested imagery.

Just as with the book and balloon, unbendable arm and hand stick, the process is a collaborative "do with" process. The client starts out deliberately imagining alongside your suggestions and ends up with a hypnotic dissociated non-volitional experience or a "hypnotic" behaving-on-purpose phenomenon that's *interpreted* as being non-volitional.

The client may have an undeniable experience that the

name is gone and discover that they can't access it.

Others have more of a both/and experience where the name is simultaneously there and not there. Some may access it, but be unable to say it. Others may say it, but do so after some struggle. Either way you can utilize the response.

The both/and borderline experience is, in my experience, more common than the full-blown experience.

Partial amnesia seems to be right at the edge of many folks' hypnotic capacity. Amnesia is for most a more difficult phenomenon to achieve than the hand stick; full-blown amnesia may be beyond most people's experience.

A Case of Bulimia

Jane was a woman in her mid-twenties who had a difficult relationship to food. More precisely, a difficult relationship to her *thoughts* around food. She would fixate on food, fixate on both "must" and "must not" ideas. This resulted in periods of "perfection" followed by binging and puking.

We worked on prescribing her symptom loops and exposing her musturbatory tendency using the formats described in this book.

However I'm convinced that it was the strategic use of name amnesia that provided the biggest felt experience-based *insight*, which then became a solid foundation for the rest of our work together. The use of name amnesia was the spontaneous utilization of a marked-out statement that she gave me.

Our conversation went like this.

> **Jane:** I just can't imagine letting go of my bulimia. It's been a part of me for so long that it feels like me.

When Jane said this, her state shifted.

Jørgen: You know, there is something that has been part of you for much longer than the bulimia and which is you to the core...your own name.

Jane: Ah,OK.

Jørgen: Can you imagine letting go of your own name...to the point where you *forget Jane.*

Jane: No, I don't think I could forget my own name.

Jørgen: Let's do a little mind experiment.

Jane: OK.

From here we went into the name amnesia format. It was "as real as real" to her and fried her circuits.

While her name was gone despite her attempts to find it, I said:

"If you can let go of your own name to the point where it's gone...and you didn't think you could...how easily can you imagine letting go of your bulimia...as your name returns... now."

Jørgen: So, what's your name?

Jane: Hahaha...it's Jane. That was insane.

Jørgen: And notice what it's like as you imagine letting go of that bulimia habit.

Jane: I can. It feels like something I can do.

I don't have long-term follow-up, but when I spoke to her a few weeks later she was doing well and had not engaged in any bulimia.

At no time did I do a hypnotic pre-talk or any formal hypnotic induction. One benefit of directly going for phenomena is that you can go for them right there and then, as tools for learning and discovery, in response to what the client gives you to utilize.

Phenomena are often excellent to loosen stuck perspectives, beliefs and identity statements. Furthermore, the use of cognitive strategies makes the client a deliberate agent who realizes that they "do it" instead of leaving thinking it was done to them by a hypnotist and his special powers. By the way, bulimics and anorexics who puke to lose weight are often good hypnotic subjects, while anorexics who just starve themselves are, more often than not, low in hypnotic capacity. There is quite a bit of research pointing in this direction.

HALLUCINATING A DOG

"How could you take such a risk?" That was a question several people asked me after my presentation/performance at the Change Phenomena conference in London 2010.

Those who asked the question were referring to the fact that I spontaneously evoked both a hallucinated dog, followed by making myself invisible—both phenomena with one guy, a psychiatrist from Birmingham. I did so with no pretalk or formal induction. Neither did I use lighter phenomena first as a buildup. This was unusual to most, and they had never seen anyone "break all the rules" and go directly for advanced hypnotic phenomena such as positive and negative hallucination.

Those who do street hypnosis (which I have never done) usually start off with magnetic hands or something like the book and balloon game, both of which utilize the ideomotor effect. If the participant doesn't respond well, there is little point in continuing, but otherwise the hypnotist might proceed with some induction and go for easy phenomena such as unbendable arm or eye catalepsy.

Then it might be some suggestion that they will find their arm levitation to be hysterically funny.

The next suggestion might be some version of amnesia.

After amnesia come the positive and negative hallucination, bizarre post-hypnotic suggestions and other severely altered realities with the absence of reality testing. Both street and stage hypnosis follow this sequence (mostly) as does

141

X
LEFT LOOKERS
EYE ROLL

formal hypnotizability testing in the lab. But the truth is that the risk wasn't that great (no, there was no bribe involved). Neither does what I did require great skill. The skill set mainly consists of the ability to scan for and select a highly hypnotizable person, and the congruence to pull it off.

I was undecided on what I wanted to do on the day of the event and still didn't know when I began my presentation. During a break earlier in the day, a psychiatrist approached me and said he had enjoyed my book, *Provocative Hypnosis*. I enjoyed our conversation and we had a great rapport.

I noticed that when he described experiences he was passionate and seemed to "go there". When I described experiences he also appeared to easily get absorbed.

This is of course no guarantee that someone will be a great hypnotic subject, but it's a good sign.

He spoke quickly, energetically and did a lot of clear eye accessing cues up and to the left.

This capacity for vivid visualization combined with the skills at absorption suggested that he might be a candidate for hypnotic hallucinations. Two other cues—both having to do with his eyes—suggested solid hypnotic capacity. Both seem to suggest that hypnotizability is a biological trait/ability. The first cue was that he frequently looked up to his left. When asked questions that require some reflection, people seem to have strong tendencies for their eyes to either swing to the left or to the right. The folks who are good at absorption into suggested imagery tend to be "left lookers". This pattern is strong for right-handed males. The consistent "right lookers" tend to be low in hypnotic capacity.

The second eye cue was that he had a high eye roll. I deliberately tested his eye roll by having him look up as high as he could, then slowly close his eyelids down as he kept looking up. The purpose is to see to what extent the sclera becomes visible and the eyes roll up into his head. My new psychiatrist friend's eyes rolled up into his head in impressive fashion.

Herbert Spiegel was the first guy to propose that the eye roll is linked to hypnotic capacity, and he documented the relationship with several thousand clients. It started in the early sixties when he had a client that was a hypnotic virtuoso. Spiegel noticed the spontaneous high eye roll.

The next day he had a patient who showed zero hypnotic capacity. Out of curiosity he tested the patient's eye roll and discovered that the patient couldn't roll his eyes at all. Intrigued, to discover if there was a pattern, he tested thousands of patients in the years to follow and documented his research. High eye rolls seem correlated with high hypnotic ability, medium eye roll with medium capacity and low eye roll with little hypnotic capacity. Spiegel claims that these correlations are about 75% accurate in actual practice since there are many factors that may inhibit a person's ability to access and use their hypnotic talent.

The findings are controversial, though and no-one has yet replicated his findings.

After reading about Spiegel and his work about ten years ago, I spent about six months testing eye rolls on clients. The difference was that I would test their eye roll *after* the hypnotic work to ensure that my expectations didn't get set beforehand. While it's far from perfect correlation, I found Spiegel's claims more accurate than not.

While Spiegel didn't make a distinction between a deliberate eye roll and a spontaneous one, the latter seems to me more connected with hypnotic talent. I have seen clients with moderate eye rolls display high *spontaneous* eye rolls.

When I first got exposed to hypnosis, as a part of my NLP studies, the whole thing seemed bogus to me—a case of role-playing and compliance. Still, I remember vividly the day I discovered that hypnosis was for real.

During an Elman induction (Dave Elman's classic) my

client's eyes rolled up into his head when I instructed him to open and close his eyes. The guy looked like he was in a much-altered state of consciousness compared to his "normal" state. He could do any suggested phenomena and described the state as very different from anything he had experienced before.

While the "rolling eyes up into the head" doesn't happen with all highs during an Elman induction, I can't think of a single case when the spontaneous eye roll during an induction didn't equate with the client being highly hypnotizable. Dave Elman pointed out that when the eyes rolled up into the head, it was a sign of hypnosis taking place.

As a contrast with Spiegel, Elman claimed everyone was hypnotizable.

Personally, I agree with Spiegel, and if there is one thing that decades of hypnotizability testing has shown, it's that people are not equally hypnotizable. Why that is so and to what extent hypnotic capacity can be improved is where the disagreement lies.

Back to the highly hypnotizable psychiatrist at the Change Phenomena conference.

James Tripp, who was also presenting, used the guy to demonstrate what he refers to as a card stick. It's like the hand stick except that the subject's fingers are stuck around a card. During that quick experience I noticed something that is very common with hypnotic virtuosos—as a result of getting so absorbed into suggested experience there is often a kind of sluggishness in responding to external cues when the suggestion is given that they reorient back to normal.

The psychiatrist needed some time to reorient back to normal. Spiegel writes about this in the book *Trance and Treatment*. Specifically, how highs can get so absorbed into a play or movie that when the curtain goes down they need a few seconds to reorient and realize that they're actually sitting in a theatre.

Those who spoke of the great risk were blind to this stuff. As I said, the main skill lies in framing the context and selecting the right subject.

During my lecturing a woman asked a question about anchoring, so I decided to "steal" the hypnosis that James had done earlier. I looked at the psychiatrist and asked him if he would be willing to demonstrate some deep trance phenomena. He said yes.

I then gestured for him to stand up and as he stood up I simply said, "And as you stand up (as he was standing up)... for each step you take...(gesturing for him to move forward) towards me...the deeper that trance becomes."

I guess you would call that the induction—he looked to be in an altered state.

I gestured for him to stand in the exact same spot that he was in when he did the card stick with James. I also raised his arm and put it in the same spot as it had been during the card stick. This is the use of spatial anchoring and an implied directive to go into the same state as he was in when he was briefly there with James. Here I was "stealing" the hypnosis and hijacking it. So far, he was responding well.

The hallucination was evoked through indirect suggestion. "You are standing here...my questions for you are...what size, breed and color is that dog *there* (pointing to a spot on the floor)?" You could see his spine straighten and pupils dilate as he started describing the dog.

"Now...when I snap my fingers, the dog gets twice as big."

He was instructed to close his eyes and given the suggestion that when he next opened his eyes, I would be invisible.

He opened his eyes and when I moved out of his field of vision his eyes didn't move an inch. That's how you know that you've got a genuine negative hallucination going. I added the suggestion that when I snapped my fingers he could see my head, but my body would be invisible. He had an amusing time with this one and so did the audience.

You can watch this demo at my website www.tilstandsterapi.com.

You can also view both James's and my presentations on the 2010 Change Phenomena DVDs.

If you watch these, I invite you to look for the various cues I described.

Oh, to give credit where credit is due, the advanced student will identify the way I elicited the visual hallucination as Milton Erickson's surprise induction. I have used this induction on a few occasions to evoke hallucinations from clients.

ENHANCING HYPNOTIZABILITY

"Anthony is hallucinating now. He can do visual hallucinations." I can't remember who told me this, but I do remember the excitement when I heard it. This was huge.

Anthony Jacquin is a skilled and knowledgeable hypnosis professional, who, along with Kevin Sheldrake, is the one who arranged the previously mentioned Change Phenomena conference.

In ordinary life, the news that someone is hallucinating dogs (and who knows what else) invisible to everyone else, and talking about it with excitement, is not considered good news. In the context of hypnosis, though, there are few things that could be better news. Anthony, just like me, has always pretty much sucked as a hypnotic subject. Those of us who watch our highly hypnotizable clients do stuff with hypnosis that we, despite our best efforts, just can't do are often simultaneously happy for our clients *and* a little envious.

Let's face it, there are a lot of choices and experiences available to the highs that the lows just don't have. Here are some examples:

Pain Control: Hypnosis is a lot more effective for pain management than placebo treatments.

This is true for the highly hypnotizable, but not so with those who have low hypnotic capacity.

Pain management is the area where hypnosis has the most scientific studies verifying its effectiveness. When used with highs, hypnosis has been used to control pain even in

147

X
YAPCO
KROGER

lengthy surgeries and dental procedures, in some cases more effectively than any form of anesthesia. In one study of pain induced in the laboratory (ischemic pain, produced by a tourniquet reducing blood flow to the forearm, and cold-pressor pain, produced by immersing the hand in ice water), hypnosis was found to be more effective in reducing reported pain than morphine, diazepam, aspirin, acupuncture or placebos (Stern *et al*, 1977).

The vast number of studies showing how hypnosis works a lot better for highs than placebo, but not for the lows (where results have a tendency to be equal), poses a problem for the socio-cognitive view and suggests a more trait and/or state-based explanation.

Consider the work of James Esdaile, a Scottish surgeon serving in India before the introduction of chemical anesthesia. Esdaile documented 345 surgeries, including amputations and removal of 70-pound scrotal tumors, with hypnosis as the sole anesthetic. Also remarkable was that his patients had only a fraction of the complications (mortality, post-surgical infections, bleeding) of others undergoing similar surgeries at the time.

Those who want details of the scientific findings regarding hypnotic analgesia and anesthesia are referred to Michael Yapko's excellent book, *Trance Work* (4th Edition).

I'm not aware of any other book that comes close in showing the scientific documentation of hypnosis with regards to various medical and psychological issues.

The skeptical (and curious) reader who wants to see a demo or two of what's possible with a skilled hypnosis professional with a good hypnotic subject should check out the DVD sold with the revised edition of William Kroger's book *Clinical and Experimental Hypnosis*. Here Kroger demonstrates hypnosis in the management of pain during labor and delivery plus surgical repair following the birth. The DVD also includes a thyroidectomy performed on a young woman with hypnosis as the sole anesthetic.

Outside of pain management there are studies showing that both cognitive behavioral therapy and psychodynamic approaches are more effective, for most participants, when combined with hypnosis.

From my own direct experience involving 16 years as an agent of change, I have over time noticed that hypnotic capacity matters. NLP techniques are, in my experience, more effective when done in hypnosis.

As long as people have at least a mid-range hypnotic capacity, it's a lot easier to work with phobias. The exception would be with exposure therapy, and while that's an effective approach, in my experience affect bridge "regression" is more effective as long as a mid-range capacity for hypnosis is present.

When it comes to issues such as allergies, asthma, migraine headaches and other psychosomatic symptoms, my results have been a lot better using hypnosis than without.

So hearing that Anthony was hallucinating dogs was exciting news for several reasons. First of all, if there was a way to take folks with low hypnotic capacity, such as Anthony and me, and turn us into hypnosis virtuosos, that would make available to the rest of us the choices already available to the highly hypnotizable. Heck, if we could just take those with zero or low capacity and train them to have mid-range capacities, then our work and client results would improve. In all my years of intense client work and experimentation I have never been able to train lows into highs.

A second reason for my excitement is that there doesn't seem to be too much innovation these days in the hypnosis field. Sure, some interesting experiments are being done combining hypnosis and neuroscience, but not many practical applications.

Thirdly, perhaps I could experience some of the wild stuff I had assisted so many of my clients in experiencing.

I had some interesting conversations with both Anthony and Kevin; it turned out they had discovered the work of the late Nicholas Spanos. Spanos was a strong proponent of the socio-cognitive view, and between 1979 and 1988 he authored or co-authored 89 papers on hypnosis, which was 7% of the 1267 written on the topic in that period.

Spanos claimed that hypnotizability could be enhanced through his Carleton Skills Training Program. In one of the studies at his lab he reported that 80% of low hypnotizability subjects were reclassified as highs after the program. Across several such studies he never claimed less than 50% of lows scoring as highs after his program.

These were remarkable claims. Especially considering how stable a trait hypnotizability had been shown to be through decades of testing even after time intervals of 25 years. The fact that previous attempts of enhancing hypnotizability had not been successful contrasted with Spanos's claim that it could be done in 75 minutes. Well that's exciting and sometimes means that someone has revolutionized a field by shaking up some fundamental assumptions.

Bandler and Grinder with their five-minute phobia cure come to mind. A seemingly preposterous claim at a time when exposure therapy, both painful and *very* time consuming, was thought of as the only thing that consistently worked. Guess what? Even if the NLP phobia cure is a bit over-hyped, NLP's founders were correct. Anyone willing to invest some time can verify this through their own direct experience. Their process works consistently well as promised. I'm still puzzled that psychologists go around pretending that it isn't so. The only reasons that make sense to me are that psychologists are paid by the hour, so are financially rewarded for incompetence. To that you can add conformity, in-group loyalty and "not invented here" syndrome.

Anyway, the program that Spanos developed for enhancing hypnotic responsiveness consists of three parts.

1. Presentation of positive information and elimination of misconceptions around hypnosis.

Nothing special about this component. Any hypnotic pre-talk is usually intended to build expectancy, eliminate fears and misconceptions. This is standard.

2. Emphasis on becoming imaginatively absorbed into the suggestion given.

This is also rather common.

3. Detailed instructions concerning how to interpret specific suggestions coupled with practicing behavioral response to such suggestions.

Clearly, it's this third component that is unique and different from other programs. Spanos has rejected the idea of dissociation being responsible for the non-volitional responses.

This third component was developed based upon a very different premise: Hypnotic suggestions are usually worded in a way that the responses will "just happen" in a non-volitional way. The hypnotist may say, "When you open your eyes the number 4 will be gone."

According to Spanos, high-susceptibles tend to treat such suggestions as tacit requests to bring about suggested responses, which they then interpret as events happening to them rather than as action they carry out. Low subjects interpret the suggestions to mean that they should passively wait for the behaviors and experiences to occur (Spanos, *et al*, 1986).

According to this view, the way to turn lows into highs

is to change their interpretation. Make it clear that they are to deliberately behave the way they are instructed to, get absorbed into the suggested reality and then interpret this enactment as subjectively real and involuntary.

Here is an example of how Spanos would train his subjects: "The suggestion will specifically tell you that your arm is like a hollow balloon being pumped up with helium...and that it's raising into the air by itself...you must do everything required of someone making believe such a thing...*you must lift your arm up*, and you must imagine that the arm is really a hollow balloon that is being pumped full of helium, raising by itself. You must...actually make it seem real.... Rivet your attention on the hollow arm, the lightness, the fact that it's going up by itself and so on. Don't imagine anything or pay attention to anything that is unrelated to the make-believe situation" (Spanos, *et al*, 1986).

After making practice runs of various suggestions, the subjects are exposed to a tape-recorded demonstration of a young woman who had first scored as a low, but has learned the cognitive skills to respond successfully. After the information and training, the subjects are tested.

On the phone, Anthony told me that the first thing to do was to lower one's standards, to settle for a both/and partial hallucination. He had started off by imagining a dog (or was it a cat?) in his peripheral vision and attempting to make it real. Then he had begun to imagine that he wasn't imagining it—that it was there all by itself and he wasn't doing it. Suddenly, it happened—he had the experience that the dog was there and it "just happened". Rather than the full-blown experience, it was an experience of it being real and knowing it's not real at the same time.

Kevin and Anthony put together something they call the Automatic Imagination model and introduced it in an interesting product called *Ripped Apart*.

I started experimenting with enhancing hypnotizability using Spanos's concepts.

Unfortunately, I disagree with Spanos as well as Anthony Jacquin and Kevin Sheldrake. In my experience it can be a useful way for some to access hypnotic phenomena, but for the most part I think it gets people to behave in a compliant way as well as to reinterpret volitional experiences as if they were non-volitional.

The psychologist and hypnosis researcher Kenneth Bowers makes an excellent point when he says that Spanos fails to make a distinction between "achieving a purpose" and "behaving on purpose". I think Bowers is correct in pointing out that hypnotic experiences are both purposeful and non-volitional, but I have been able to develop a couple of practical applications for change work based on what Anthony and Kevin shared with me.

I noticed that what we are attempting to do with the Automatic Imagination Model is to take a volitional cognitive act and turn it into a non-volitional experience, or at least interpret it in this way. It's the exact opposite approach of the one I use when doing symptom prescription. Here the client comes in and claims that they are suffering from anxiety or depression. The implication being that these experiences "just happen" and are completely non-volitional. My intent is to help them realize that they are "doing it" and that it's an experience that they are largely creating.

Let's take a look at symptom prescription using hypnotic phenomena.

HAVING YOUR HALLUCINATION

Monica was a young woman in her mid-twenties with an interesting issue. Very often, while being engaged in some activity, she would think to herself something like, "What if X happened?" and then hallucinate X. Later she would have trouble knowing if X really did happen. She found it embarrassing and inconvenient (not to mention scary) that she had to ask her friends if X happened or if the shared consensus view they presented was reality. This young woman was an excellent hypnotic subject and could easily do hypnotic hallucinations. You could make the case that Monica was *had* by her hallucinations. Our objective was for her to *have* them instead.

We started playing with imagining a cat on the floor. I would then ask her to rate it on a 1–10 scale regarding how "real as real" it was. Then I had her imagine that she wasn't imaging it...that it was just there.

This was all it took to turn an imagined object into a hallucinated object. It got so real that it scared her a bit. She discovered that by reminding herself that it was imagined she could turn it back into an imagined object. Me being present and suggesting she could do so helped her develop the skill of turning an imagined object into a hallucinated object and then back into an imagined object.

We then did some symptom prescription where she would ask herself, "What if X happens?", imagine something, turn it into a hallucination, then turn it back into an imagined experience.

Then, as soon as she realized she was hallucinating, she would imagine a goofy-looking cat included and quickly turn the cat into a hallucinated cat. I suggested that since the cat and the other hallucination were now linked together, if she changed one, the other would change as well. Monica discovered that as soon as she reminded herself that the cat was imagined, then the rest of the hallucination changed into something that she knew that she was imagining.

Short-term feedback confirmed that she was now able to

have her hallucinations and no longer had to ask her friends if X really happened.

Linda was another client who was a great hypnotic subject with whom I explored the Automatic Imagination Model. Like Monica, she could also turn an imagined object into a hallucinated one after being told to imagine X, and then imagining that she wasn't imagining it—that it was there and just happening. She wasn't as extreme as Monica, as she could keep some reality testing going on without help from me.

Later in the session we did some hypnotic work where she would project traumatic memories onto a screen so that she could dissociate from them. However, one of the memories was so traumatic and overwhelming that she would experience the screen disappearing and find herself back in the hallucinated experience all over again.

While doing double dissociation (like the NLP phobia cure) helped, what made the difference was the Automatic Imagination Model. She was instructed to imagine a goofy-looking cat on the screen as a part of the memory and to turn it into a hallucination. I suggested that the memory would get real shortly, but that all she had to was to realize she was imagining the cat and the rest of the memory would also turn into a movie way over there.

It worked beautifully.

I should point out that both of these women had solid hypnotic capacity.

So, while my experience is *not* that it turns lows into highs, I've had some use for this approach as a metaphorical teaching tool and at times as a useful tool in symptom prescription.

There seem to be different processes at work here to elicit hypnotic phenomena. On the one hand we have deliberate cognitive strategies at play with the hand stick, name amnesia and Automatic Imagination Model. There is a deliberate cognitive strategy of "thinking, feeling, behaving", with the suggestions resulting in either a dissociated response and/or a purposeful behavior interpreted as non-volitional. It's not necessarily that black and white, and likely there is a scale of experience.

On the other hand we have the way I evoked a feeling of attraction with Sara and the positive and negative hallucinations with the psychiatrist. Here I used indirect suggestion and these phenomena were most likely the result of dissociation and not conscious cognitive strategies.

Another way to think of it would be to label them "top down" phenomena (cognitive strategies) and "bottom up" phenomena (dissociation). My current thinking is that phenomena created with low-to-mid range capacity are probably more top-down while medium-to-high and virtuoso experiences are more likely to result from a bottom-up approach.

Of course this is too tidy, and my strong recommendation is that you get flexible with your suggestion artistry as well as your frameworks. As philosopher, trader and author Nassim Taleb is fond of saying, "Ideology is fairytales for adults."

I have had clients with whom a hypnosis frame with an Elman induction and suggestions for amnesia has not worked, but an "imagination game" frame combined with a top-down cognitive approach (á la Tripp's name amnesia) has worked wonders.

I have also had the opposite happen. At a seminar last year in Amsterdam, the majority of the participants developed amnesia for suggestions during a group induction where I used primarily indirect suggestion. Here, direct Elman-style approaches and cognitive strategies didn't work quite as well. One woman did not respond to the top-down name amnesia piece at all. However, after an Elman induction she could easily develop amnesia for numbers. Name amnesia was a no go despite me working quite hard to get it.

A bit later my good friend Brian Mahoney, who was

assisting me, was able to finally get name amnesia after linking her name with a funny song.

Another participant could do a convincing unbendable arm but no amnesia or hallucinations except when he used the Automatic Imagination Model. He could hallucinate the smell of a dog very convincingly despite not being able to hallucinate the sound or image of a dog.

REAL HALLUCINATIONS

My own direct experience doing hypnosis, especially affect bridge memory reconstruction hypnotherapy, has convinced me that hypnosis cannot be completely explained by socio-cognitive models.

Back in 2004 I worked with a highly hypnotizable woman named Rita, who had basilar migraine headaches on a consistent basis and had for years. Consciously, she was convinced that they were caused by the grief she felt since her mother's death many years prior.

I used affect bridge memory reconstruction work with Rita. This is sometimes called a version of hypnotic age regression, but I don't use the term "regression" since people aren't really regressing during hypnotic work.

Since I described this process in detail, in my book *Provocative Hypnosis*, I won't repeat myself here.

The simple steps are:

- Isolate the main context in which the symptom occurs.

- Use a hypnosis frame.

- Talk about the reconstructive function of memory.

- Elicit the client's timeline and do a "practice run".

157

- Establish visual anchors with position 1 as in the event, position 2 as above the event and position 3 as above and before the event looking towards now.

- Do a hand drop induction.

- Evoke the emotion behind the symptom.

- Use the emotion as an affect bridge as far as it goes back in time.

- Update the reconstructed memories that appear.

- Test the work and future-pace.

I'd like to invite you to see a live demo of me working with a woman named Saskia in April 2012 at a Provocative Hypnosis course I did in Amsterdam, Holland. You can find the video demo at www.provocativehypnosis.com as well as www.tilstandsterapi.com.

The demo lasts for 23 minutes. Saskia was struggling mightily with asthma. A follow-up at a seminar one year later confirmed that she had reduced her symptoms and her medication by about half. Just as interesting was that a severe phobia spontaneously vanished as well. She didn't tell me about the phobia, nor did she have any idea that it was somehow connected to her asthma.

Two things happened that almost always accompany successful affect bridge work.

- The unconscious selects the emotion to work with, and it emerges in a non-volitional manner. Quite regularly it's a different emotion than the client suspected.

- The reconstructed memory that comes up is *not* the event that the client may consciously have attributed her symptoms to. It's always without exception an earlier memory construct, and the client is surprised by what emerges.

Often they will say something to the effect of, "I haven't thought about *that* in decades," or "I had no idea that memory was connected with this issue."

My direct experience has been, time and time again, that when the unconscious selects the memory construct to work with, the results are better than when someone using their conscious mind selects some memory to work with.

I have also noticed that this type of work is a lot more effective when a hypnotic induction is used. In the beginning I would do straight timeline therapy as taught by Tad James. With James's format there isn't much of a hypnotic induction. I noticed that my results got better when I began to do an Elman induction before the timeline work.

However, what really turned the effectiveness up was when I began to use a hand drop induction, then went straight for the emotion. This allowed those with low hypnotic capacity to make the most of their hypnotic talents.

While Rita did have some grief come up, what emerged first was rage connected to some early memory constructs. She also had spontaneous amnesia for most of the process. As I sit here writing this, in January 2014, Rita hasn't had a single migraine headache since our session back in 2004.

Rita displayed the characteristics that Herbert Spiegel observed were the norm with the most highly hypnotizable— people with amazing capacities for absorption, dissociation and suggestibility.

- The ability to do positive and negative hallucinations.

- The ability to do "age regression" in the present tense.

- The ability to experience suggested or spontaneous amnesia for most or all of the session.

Levi, the stepson of Wayne Marsh, is a great example. Wayne has promoted several seminars with me in the UK and at one of these Levi asked if I could help him with his vision.

We did a formal induction, some "regression" and some direct suggestions to correct his nearsightedness.

I suggested that he not only have amnesia for the session, but that he would be amnesic to the fact that we had even worked on the issue. I further suggested that he had just closed his eyes and had a massage from the massage chair.

Several interesting things happened after he reoriented. I asked him if the massage was good and he confirmed that it was. It soon became clear that he had complete amnesia for us having worked on his nearsightedness.

He spontaneously reported being able to see better. I've got to admit that I don't know if these were genuine improvements in vision or just a feeling that his vision had improved.

Later in the seminar I attempted to evoke a positive hallucination of a nude movie star and failed. He was genuinely sorry that he hadn't been able to be hypnotized and for embarrassing me in front of the audience.

This was the huge convincer for a few NLP-trained folks who could see that Levi was being sincere and therefore concluded that the session he had amnesia for had real results.

His amnesia was solid, as several seminar participants discovered when they attempted to hint at our session without getting anywhere with Levi.

During practice time Levi was hypnotized by a couple of not-so-skilled participants, and they could not get hallucinations from him.

The big finale came a couple of days later when Wayne showed Levi the recording of our session. First he negatively hallucinated himself when watching the session. Then, once he realized it was him, he got a headache and ran out of the room a bit freaked out. Interestingly, in that moment, the gains—whether he actually saw better or just felt that he did—instantly vanished.

These are a few examples from my work showing that I think/suggest we need—in addition to a socio-cognitive angle—a trait/state model to do hypnosis more justice.

Let's leave my experience and look at what neuroscience has to say.

In a study (Kosslyn, Thompson, Constantini-Ferrando, Alpert, Spiegel), hypnotized (and highly hypnotizable) subjects given the instruction to hallucinate color while viewing black and white photographs had the part of the brain used for color processing "light up" in brain scans. The same brain regions showed decreased activity when they were instructed to hallucinate draining color from color images. This did not happen when low hypnotizables were involved.

These findings in highs show strong neurophysiological processes at play during hypnosis and suggest that imagination and role-taking aren't sufficient as an explanation. The researchers concluded that hypnosis is a psychological state with distinct neural correlates. High hypnotizables tend to have greater cognitive flexibility, more focused attention involving the frontal attentional system, and a great capacity for emotional arousal (Crawford, 1989).

Something similar happens when the highly hypnotizable (in a study by Szechtman, et al) were asked to hallucinate while in a PET (position emission tomography) scanner. First they heard a recording of the line "the man did not speak often, but when he did, it was worth hearing what he had to say". Then they followed instructions to imagine hearing this line again, or they listened while the hypnotist suggested that the tape was playing once more, although it was not. The result was an auditory hallucination amongst the subjects. The PET scan revealed that the subjects' right anterior cingulated cortex was just as active when they were hallucinating as when they were actually hearing the line. This did not happen when the subjects were merely *imagining* the line. Clearly, hypnosis had stimulated the area of the brain to register the hallucinated voice as real.

De-automating the Automatic (Raz, et al, 2005) demonstrated that post-hypnotic suggestions given to the highly hypnotizable helped them dramatically reduce Stroop interference when exposed to the Stroop effect.

The Stroop effect is based on the work of John Ridley Stroop. It involves having a subject report the color of letters that appear in words—red written in a blue font, yellow written in a green font, green written in red and blue written in yellow, etc. When the subjects look at a word, they see both its color and its meaning. If these two pieces of evidence are in conflict, they have to make a choice. Because experience has taught them that word meaning is more important than ink color, interference occurs when they try to attend only to the ink color. The interference effect suggests a person is not always in control of attention.

Raz (the guy who did the experiment) points out, "It's an effect that takes place even if you do not want it to happen. Reading words is a deeply ingrained process. It's automatic for people who are proficient readers.... Reporting the ink color instead of the color word you are reading creates conflict and that translates into more errors on incongruent words. It also translates into slower reaction time or a decrease of speed. These two factors—more errors and slower reaction time characterize the Stroop effect" (Parsons-Fein, 2006).

What Raz did was to divide subjects into low-and high-hypnotizability groups. During hypnosis the subjects were given post-hypnotic suggestions instructing them that when exposed to the Stroop test, they would construe the words as nonsense strings. These suggestions resulted in the highs viewing the Stroop words as nonsense foreign signs.

162

As a result, this group scored much higher on being able to separate the words from the colors.

Raz commented on this research and its implications: "What my research findings suggest is that hypnosis can de-automate certain processes for some people. That says something of the ability of the brain, or the higher brain functions, to override and exert top-down control over other brain regions that are probably responsible for the practiced event...and that may imply that we can take habitual behavior, or all kind of behavioral patterns, and potentially modify them.... Words can translate into specific influences on focal brain regions, which is news—big news" (Parsons-Fein, 2006).

Arguments for dissociation.

To me, while both may be labeled hypnotic, there seems to be a big difference between Jane's name amnesia and the sort of amnesia that Levi experienced.

With Jane, the amnesia was produced in a "top-down" manner using cognitive strategies where the end result was experienced as non-volitional. You could call it a successful attempt at forgetting.

Levi's amnesia could more accurately be described as a failed attempt to remember something. Furthermore I suspect that there was no cognitive strategy involved.

Jane's amnesia will work as long as she deliberately stays in the hypnotic loop. Levi's amnesia held up no matter where he directed his conscious attention until he saw the video of himself being hypnotized.

To me, this suggests dissociation as a main mechanism, and there is some science to support this view.

Bowers and Woody (1996) noticed that highs who were

163

given instructions to stop thinking about their favorite automobile were able to do so. Some couldn't remember what car it was at all, and on average the rest reported that the thought would occur less than once every two minutes. Non-hypnotizable subjects, who were not hypnotized, reported that the unwanted thought occurred over three times per minute.

Ruehle and Zamansky (1997) gave hypnotized and hypnosis-simulating subjects the suggestion to forget the number 11 and replace it with 12 while they did addition problems. Hypnotized subjects were faster than simulators at doing the task under these conditions.

M. E. Miller (1986) did a very interesting experiment with the intent to find out if high-level cognitive work was required to produce hypnotic analgesia. If it were, that should diminish the available resources for performing a demanding cognitive task at the same time. This should be the case even if the cognitive effort is hidden from consciousness by an amnesia-like barrier. However if instead suggestion activates a sub-system for pain control through dissociation, this should not be the case.

Eighteen highs and eighteen lows were selected for experiments combining pain due to having their arms immersed in ice-cold water with cognitively demanding reading assignments.

Participants were either hypnotized and administered suggestions for hypnotic analgesia, or instructed to use various cognitive strategies they had just learned to cope with cold-pressor pain.

Both the cognitive strategies and hypnotic suggestions were a lot more effective for highs than for lows. There was also no difference between the cognitive strategies and hypnotic analgesia for the highs. However, the test showed that hypnotic analgesia didn't interfere with the reading test while the cognitive strategies did. Performance declined about 35%

during the first (pre-treatment) immersion in the cold pressor.

In addition, for both lows and highs in the cognitive strategy condition there was an extra drop of about 30% in their reading performance from pre- to post-treatment immersion in the cold pressor.

Let's turn to the hypnotic analgesia group. The lows reported just about an 8% decline under the same conditions. Remarkably, the highs showed a 10% increase in their reading performance. This strongly suggests that hypnotic analgesia does not depend on high level cognitive resources and is due to dissociation.

I hope this chapter on hypnosis has not only given you some ideas around how you can use hypnotic phenomena to help clients gain perspective, but also that it has given you more ideas about your own perspectives around hypnosis. The ability to use multiple frameworks—even when they seem contradictory—based on client needs and contextual factors, will likely increase both your effectiveness and enjoyment when engaged in change artistry.

EXPECTATION ABSOLUTISM

One snowy morning a client found me shoveling snow out-side my office. It turned out that he had arrived a week ear-ly for our scheduled appointment. It didn't really matter though, because he didn't need a full session—all it took for him to change was to catch a glimpse of me shoveling snow.

I had seen this client a couple of years previously for some phobias and social anxiety issues. Our work was successful. However, in the weeks prior to our appointment he had be-gan to do anxiety again. Nowhere near the intensity of the previous symptoms, but still enough to be bothersome. Sub-sequent follow-up established that all it took was seeing me shoveling snow. As he said, "As soon as I saw you, I knew that I was going to be OK."

More recently, a woman called me requesting help with what she described as severe claustrophobia. She had mas-tered the art of phobicking so well that recently, while in the shower, she panicked and wrecked the shower cabinet. Due to both of us having busy schedules we weren't able to book an appointment earlier than a month or so later.

A few days before our scheduled appointment she called me and said she was convinced that she didn't need to see me. Her phobic reactions had simply vanished. She told me that something I had said on the phone had made her realize that she could change, and she did.

I often chuckle inside when "skeptics" huff and puff with disdain, hostility and downright contempt when they hear

TASKING

stories about people making huge changes in one session. I have had so many clients make such "impossible" changes, before even setting foot in my office, that I have lost track of how many a long time ago. The time between booking the appointment and showing up at the office can be magical.

These changes showcase the power of expectation; change artistry has a lot to do with expectation management. The first client, the one who saw me shoveling snow, already knew how to change. I think seeing me was simply a reminder, an anchor that reminded him that he had changed previously and therefore he could do it again.

The shower-wrecking client clearly knew how to do phobias as well as how to undo them. She may not have known that she had those capacities before I said something that helped her have an insight that enabled her to believe that she could and would change.

Thank god these pre-session changes aren't the norm, otherwise I would be completely broke. What's more common is that some clients make progress on their goal between booking the appointment and showing up. You can't order these types of changes, but you can create an overall context that makes it more likely that those changes occur.

One factor is your ability to address your client's fears and frustrations over the phone to such an extent, that they believe and expect change to occur. Both your confidence and competence are important pieces of the puzzle.

Another biggie is tasking clients with assignments before the first session. These can be tasks designed to build relevant skills and/or tasks to build commitment. We observe our behaviors and tell stories about what our behavior means. A client who observes himself doing tasks over time is likely to conclude, based on observing his own behavior, that he is committed to change.

In my opinion one of the biggest mistakes an agent of

change can make is to allow his clients to just show up cold at the office. This is way too common an occurrence for hypnotherapists who often think (and communicate) that the changes happen exclusively while the client is in a hypnotic state. Few are more aware of the power of expectation and belief than those skilled at hypnosis. This can be something of a double-edged sword when hypnotherapists oversell and over-promise.

To some extent we are playing a confidence game. The confident (as perceived by client) hypnotherapist who expects the client to change will communicate those expectations on many levels. Since they know that rapid change is possible, and that client expectation often plays a big part, they often end up putting all their eggs in one basket.

After the first session there are four possible outcomes. Let's use a phobia client as an example:

1. Complete change

   The phobia is gone and the result has been confirmed by real life testing.

2. Improvement

   This may be anything from a small shift to someone who is almost there.

3. No change

   The client reports that the session, and what you did together, had no effect whatsoever.

4. Symptom increase

   The client reports that his phobia or symptom has gotten worse.

You don't have to spend a lot of time in this profession before you experience all these client outcomes.

The main lesson is this: You need a functional framework

that ensures that you can utilize all four responses, and where you still have trust and credibility even if the third or fourth outcome occurs.

If you go around pumping yourself up as "the hypnotist" and tell your client that you can hypnotize anyone, that change is easy, and that all your clients change quickly, then you're screwed unless you get outcome number 1 and perhaps number 2 with some goodwill.

Chances are that the client won't even contact you, and perversely enough, the inner press secretary can write that off as another success by spinning a story of how the client must have gotten what he wanted, otherwise he would have called.

While outcome number 4 is relatively rare it does occur. This is why you don't want to book people for single sessions, not even for phobias.

You may just have opened the lid on Pandora's Box and you'd better have a follow-up scheduled for your client. Imagine what it's like for a client to expect his phobia to vanish in one session—largely based on the framing of a hypnotherapist—only to discover that he is more afraid *after* the session. If you were that client, how much credibility would that hypnotherapist or NLP coach have for you?

By the way, if I could choose between a client having "no change" or "getting worse", I would choose the client "getting worse". At least that means what we are doing is stirring things up.

The art of expectation management lies in allowing miracles while simultaneously encouraging expectations that are positive and realistic. And, as previously mentioned, setting things up in such a way that responses 3 and 4 can be utilized as a result of you still being credible to the client.

I schedule two consultations with most of my clients. In my experience that is sufficient for most clients most of the time. I tell them this and also inform them that some clients require additional sessions.

I usually say something along these lines: "After the first session there are four possible outcomes. Maybe half are done after one session. Around 35% have made solid improvements. A few report no change and even fewer increase their symptom. But which of these categories you're in after the first session isn't important. The important thing is that you and I have a commitment to work until we get it resolved.

"There are two types of clients out there when there is some issue. Client A goes out and discovers that he is still afraid. He doesn't really do anything productive and if he calls, often weeks or months later, it's to say it didn't work. Client A doesn't succeed.

"Client B goes out and discovers he is still afraid. He calls me immediately, says he is still afraid, and asks what our next step is. Client B almost always succeeds.

"I only work with those in category B. Are you willing to commit to that?"

I lean back, shut up and wait for the client to commit or not.

As you can see I am projecting a role for them to enact. Once they say "yes" they are more likely to behave in a way that's consistent with that role.

While expectations are important, they aren't the only game in town. In the context of hypnosis I have had clients with high expectations and little capacity and vice versa.

Sometimes the client has unrealistic expectations and the last thing you want to do is to leave those unchallenged. One common example is the client who has a family member who has made dramatic changes in one session, and now they are calling and ordering the same outcome for themselves. This implies that what they bring to the table doesn't matter. The problem is that it *does* matter. They don't necessarily have the same level of motivation and commitment. They may not have the same hypnotic capacity, nor the same capacity for perspective-taking, etc. I point this out to them and bluntly tell them that those who change in one session are usually the ones not very concerned with time and who are willing to do whatever it takes.

ROLE PROJECTION FOR THE STORYTELLER

Clients often have the mistaken notion that their job is to come in and tell their story and that your job is to be understanding and empathetic. Unfortunately, many psychologists play the "empathic" role and project the "babbling victim" role onto their clients.

The last thing you want is an empathetic change artist. The agent of change doesn't understand his clients; neither does he "feel their pain".

If the client talks about issues with his father, and the therapist attempts to understand, he will do so by accessing images, thoughts and feelings based on his own personal history. But these feelings have nothing to do with the client and everything to do with the therapist.

The more he attempts to understand, the more the change work revolves around him and not the client. Nor does the therapist "feel your pain". The therapist imagines what it would be like, feels his *own* pain, and projects that onto the client. With a little luck he will be in as un-resourceful a state as the client, doing therapy on himself under the guise of helping his client and charging for the privilege.

The therapist who views the client through the filter of his own projected pain will be much less resourceful than if he could simply be present and available.

The great change artists and therapists do care about

their clients, but they don't do sympathy or empathy. Rather they have good boundaries and use compassion. When I talk about compassion I mean goodwill towards the other person, and an insight into the structure of experience as well as the likely state and mindset behind the client's symptomatic behavior. When I work with a client with serious anger issues who may have beaten his wife or child, I don't go into the same states they do. I don't "feel their pain" at all. I listen in a very present and focused mode. I demonstrate competence by saying stuff that gives them the *illusion* that I understand them. My verbalizations are about the structure of their experience and the rather impersonal nature of their issue. I know that the angering client is likely to be engaging in musturbatory thinking, he is likely to believe in his own thinking, likely to think that events and people piss him off and likely to damn both himself and others. Furthermore, angering clients focus on the crappy behaviors of others and the perceived effect it has on them instead of being compassionate and recognizing the other person's "innocence" in believing in his thoughts and operating out of a crappy state.

I help the clients realize these things and make sure to demonstrate non-absolutism, unconditional self- and other-acceptance as well as compassion. There is no place for sympathy or empathy here.

Back to the storytelling client: The lousy change artist will wallow in content misery with the client and focus on events, what other people have said or done and how that makes the client feel. The client will play out the victim role and understand that his story is *right*, confirmed by an expert.

Most ethical and skilled change artists recognize that the emphasis ought to be on the client's ways of thinking and acting in the world.

If you directly emphasize the latter, especially if the client has seen psychologists who have gone the victim route, he may feel offended and think that you don't care and don't know what you're doing.

I have found the following role projection—which I use at the beginning of a session—to be of enormous value: "You know, when people come in here they often think that they are supposed to tell their story, that I should listen, and that understanding 'why' will make their issue go away. I don't work that way at all, because while clients often can feel understood, there is rarely any change. The only thing that concerns me is how you structure your own thinking and how to help you change that, so if you go into storytelling mode I will cut you off—not to be rude, but to be effective. Is that OK?"

Once they say yes, it's so much easier to work with them; the chances of them going into victim mode and story telling are reduced. If and when they do it, they are not likely to be offended or think that you don't care when you interrupt, but are inclined to think that you are doing it to help them, since that interpretation fits the frame and role relationship they have agreed to.

Don't just present the role projection and move on. Instead, ask them if they are OK with what you presented, and make sure they verbalize their agreement. Once they have verbally agreed, the principle of internal consistency kicks in and increases compliance.

Check out Robert Cialdini's classic book, *Influence*, for an in-depth understanding of this principle.

ROLE PROJECTION FOR SKEPTICS

Very few self-defined skeptics do much independent thinking. Mostly, they are establishment conformists who use their alleged skepticism to defend the paradigm they are operating out of instead of searching for approximate truth.

The paradigm they are defending is usually one they have internalized from "proper authority" in whatever field they are identified with. It's important to realize this to be able to deal effectively with self-defined skeptics.

Naturally if someone says they are skeptical of something specific I will address it directly until the client is satisfied, but I'm talking about something different here. I'm talking about the person who presents himself as a skeptic like it's an identity statement. This "skeptic" is doing a role-projection on you, and if you accept the role, chances are that both you and the client will be worse off.

The skeptic role-projection usually goes something like this: The skeptic will analyze what you say to see if it fits the world-view he or she is operating out of (many think they are objective and have no map-territory distinction), and only those things that fit within the skeptic's world-view will be considered; the rest will automatically be discarded.

Sure, the client may be operating out of a model that is easy to apply to the solving of their issue. Sometimes an inform-ational approach is all that is needed. However, quite often effective change requires a more trans-form-ational approach, one where the client is willing to use his skepticism to also challenge his own deeper assumptions and the way he understands.

When the self-defined skeptic does his identity statement I want the option of transformational work, so I offer the following role projection: "Oh, thank *god!* I haven't had a real skeptic in here for years. You're sure you're a *real* skeptic...? See, most of those who come in here and claim to be skeptical are people who have swallowed the establishment view uncritically, and if what I say doesn't fit that, then they'll automatically reject it. But that's not skepticism, that's conformity and obedience.

"A real skeptic, on the other hand, will of course question what I say, but he'll be just as skeptical of his own assumptions and willing to challenge those. And he realizes that the only way he's going to figure out what's true is to commit to having the experiences first and engaging full out and only later analyze based on the real-world results. So...are you a *real* skeptic?"

If the client agrees to this—and most accept the role—you will have a much-engaged and responsive client. He has, by accepting the role, agreed to be willing to challenge his own deeper assumptions. He has agreed to experience first and analyze later. He has agreed that the criteria for evaluation be real-life results, not if what you are asking/suggesting fits his current model of the view.

Do recognize that you are asking a lot of your client here. Those with self-sovereign minds are not "psychologically oriented" and think that they pretty much see objective reality as it is. They may think you're a trickster or over-complicator with this talk about deeper assumptions.

You may have to settle for just "testing first" to see if it works. The socialized mind you can challenge to challenge the stuff he has learned and taken for granted. The self-authored have a lot more self-reflective capacities, and the self-transforming mind can truly challenge his inner system for meaning-making.

This particular role-projection is golden, but don't take my word for it—test it out. Oh, if the client doesn't say that he is a skeptic, but you strongly get that vibe from him, you can do this as a quotes pattern: "You know, I had a client last week who came in and told me he was a skeptic, and I told him..." Then you go into the role projection. You may of course utilize embedded commands and calibrate and utilize his non-verbal responses.

BELIEVING IS SEEING

A quick look in the mirror confirmed my hunch that something wasn't quite right. As soon as I realized that my leather jacket was missing I knew immediately where I'd left it. I'm blessed with a good memory, so an image of my jacket on the back of the chair at the pizza restaurant where I'd just had dinner instantly popped into consciousness. I glanced at my watch and reckoned that if I ran through the rainy streets of London I would get to the restaurant before it closed. I made it just in time and was relieved to find that the waiter who served my food was still there. Surely he had my jacket.

I explained to him that I had forgotten my black leather jacket on the back of my chair as I pointed out the chair.

To my surprise he claimed that he hadn't seen any leather jacket and that he didn't have it.

Even worse he claimed that I wasn't wearing one while at the restaurant. At that moment I knew that something was wrong, and I was instantly suspicious. It seemed strange that he would claim with certainty that I hadn't been wearing a jacket. Who keeps track of what their customers are wearing unless it's somehow unusual? Besides, I clearly remembered exactly where I had left it.

When I kept pressing the issue he avoided eye contact and dismissed me. He was reluctant to ask the other restaurant workers about my jacket, and when he finally did, they all acted weird, as if they were uncomfortable and were hiding something. At this point I was pretty sure that someone there had stolen my jacket. My suspicion wasn't exactly reduced when I was told that the owner was on vacation. How convenient. After realizing that I had gotten screwed and there was nothing I could do about it, I started walking back towards my hotel.

At this point I was frustrated and irritated, and my mind

176

kept replaying the conversation as well as scenarios involving who had stolen my jacket. What low-life pathetic scum to
steal from their own customers! I had even tipped them well,
those bastards.

It seemed extremely unlikely that anyone but the restaurant staff could have stolen it. There was only a middle-aged
couple there when I left the restaurant the first time and
there were no customers there when I came back just before
closing time.

I was in a pretty cranky mood when I got back to the hotel,
but as I walked past the hotel bar, something happened that
rocked my world.

"Hey, mate! You left this earlier." It was the voice of the
bartender who was holding up my leather jacket.

I was stunned. I felt as if I were in an episode of *The Twi-
light Zone*. I burst out laughing. As a matter of fact, I laughed
so hard that I started crying. Understandably, the bartender
looked a bit uneasy, but after I explained what had just happened he was laughing nearly as hard as I had.

To be honest, this experience freaked me out a bit. I started doubting my own mind and even my own sanity.

Fast forward about a decade.

It was April 2012 and I was in Amsterdam to do a four-
day provocative hypnosis seminar.

I went to sleep at around midnight hoping to get a good
night's sleep the night before the seminar started. A nice
woman named Karin Louis was going to pick me up in the
lobby the following morning and drive me to the seminar location.

Holy shit...I awoke after what felt like a twelve-hour
sleeping marathon with the utter conviction that I must have
overslept. A quick glance at my watch confirmed my fear, it
was nine o'clock.

Damn, those useless bastards at the reception had forgotten my wake-up call.

I called downstairs and asked if they could see a blonde woman named Karin, perhaps she had asked for me.

When they said no I thought she was running late and asked them to tell her I would be down shortly if she showed up before I was down in the reception area.

I gave the receptionist a small lecture on the importance of actually following through on scheduled wake-up calls. Incredibly, instead of owning his mistake and apologizing, he claimed that my wake-up call wasn't until later in the morning. I remember thinking that the guy had zero sense of personal responsibility. Another quick glance at my watch, it was now three minutes past nine. I jumped in the shower, then brushed my teeth, got dressed, grabbed my briefcase and ran towards the elevators. It was now ten past nine. One thing seemed a bit odd—I noticed that it was very dark outside considering that it was both April and nine o'clock in the morning.

A couple minutes later I rushed towards the desk, and noticed that the only person there was a lone receptionist. No Karen either. Besides, it was dark outside.

I realized something was wrong. Looking up at a big clock above the reception, I saw that it was almost fifteen past *three*.

The receptionist confirmed that the big clock was indeed correct, accepted my sincere apologies and appeared rather amused by the whole spectacle. There was nothing to do but go back to sleep.

You may at this point be wondering if I am a bit insane—slightly psychotic perhaps.

However, these two experiences are just dramatic examples of something everyone does. As is often the case, almost everything we think may be evidence of something being wrong with us is simply part of the human condition.

Almost everyone believes that they arrive at their beliefs as a result of a combination of real-life experience and objective analysis and reason. If you believe that this applies to you, then my hotel adventures will seem more than a little nutty. You're most likely wrong on both accounts, another brain-created illusion. Cognitive science on the topic of belief shows that what I did is pretty much what we all do. The brain is a belief *engine*, and we actually start with the belief and then use logical analysis and reason to explain away what doesn't fit while selectively paying attention to what supports our beliefs.

Michael Shermer, author of *The Believing Brain*, argues that the process of patternicity and agenticity are basic ingredients of the "belief engine".

Patternicity refers to the fact that our brains have evolved to both detect and create patterns. Back in the day, if exposed to a sudden sound in the environment, your best shot at survival was to respond as if a predator was targeting you for lunch without sticking around to discover it might be a false alarm.

We are the descendents of those who treated all potential patterns as real. This is likely a huge factor in us being disposed to automatically see patterns everywhere.

Agenticity refers to us humans being story tellers. As story tellers we project meaning, intent and cause-effect relationships onto random events and perceived patterns.

In front of the hotel room mirror my brain immediately formed a belief that explained where my jacket was. Then my brain thought out the experience, selectively paid attention to everything that supported that belief and ignored everything else. I did more than that—I unconsciously projected the waiter/restaurant staff as thieves and interpreted everything they said and did, as well as what they didn't say and do, in a way congruent with my belief.

179

In Amsterdam, the same processes were at play. I started with a belief and that belief altered what I was actually able to see. It's quite incredible, or so it seems, that my brain, time after time made me see the watch at nine o'clock, three past nine, ten past nine, etc. when it was three o'clock, three past three, etc. An experience of "believing is seeing".

Perhaps something similar was happening in my brain to what took place in the brains of the highly hypnotizable whose color processing regions lighted up when they hallucinated color.

Consider an ex-wife or husband—how we project all sorts of wonderful qualities onto that person while in love, and then later project a completely different human being and conclude that the person has changed.

Once I believed that the receptionist had screwed up my wake-up call, my brain projected a receptionist who was irresponsible, lazy, and incompetent as well as unable to own up to his own mistake. Everything he said got interpreted in a way that fit my belief.

It was my thinking that was lazy and irresponsible, and I projected the qualities of my thinking onto the receptionist.

The amusing part is how instantly I projected very different qualities onto both the waiter and the receptionist as soon as I was "enlightened". Suddenly, they appeared to be quite reasonable, understanding and responsible, even when dealing with a difficult customer like me.

Another interesting factor here was my strong sense of certainty—my conviction that I was right. Amos Tversky and Daniel Kahneman have done research which shows that the feeling of certainty is unrelated to actual competence. Rather, the certainty seems to be the result of availability bias and internal coherence.

Availability bias has to do with how easily some piece of information comes to mind. Internal coherence has to do with being able to put together the pieces of our mental puzzle. Once the pieces of our internal puzzle fit together we have internal coherence, and then we project that internal coherence to equate with understanding something in the external world. In other words, we are map eaters who fail to make an essential map-territory distinction. We fail to distinguish between feeling that we understand something and actual competence.

According to Robert Kegan's theory of developmental psychology, one benefit of a self-transforming mind is that those who operate there are less likely to confuse internal coherence with wholeness or completeness.

Oh, something that really bugged me about these hotel adventures is how I was at the mercy of the bartender and the receptionist for the bubble to burst. There is little reason to think that I would have ever discovered my restaurant screwup without that bartender. You may be wondering if I had a few drinks at that bar. The answer is no. The only drink I purchased was a Diet Coke.

Most of us don't really get much wiser or more competent with experience, even if we are convinced that we do. As an example, psychologists do not get better (as a group) at doing psychotherapy with decades of additional experience. There is some solid research that shows that not only do they *not* improve with experience, there is no evidence that they are better than psychotherapists who don't have a psychology degree. We think (most of us) that psychologists are better at predicting which criminals will re-offend when released. In fact, they aren't better at these predictions than the "average Joe". Neither are they better at detecting lies or determining if a person charged with sexual abuse has actually committed the crime or not. If you want the science behind the claims I refer you to Robyn Dawe's excellent book *House of Cards*.

That we mindlessly assume that psychologists have these

skills, and let them act as if they do in our legal systems, has contributed to convicting the innocent on a massive scale.

Judges aren't any better either, in detecting lies or assessing guilt or innocence, than average Joe. Neither do they generally get better over time. Quite the opposite—chances are that there is a decline in their ability to predict and evaluate over time.

John Grinder has often made the point that all beliefs are limiting. That as soon as we believe something we have the strong tendency to see what supports the belief and ignore all the stuff that doesn't and that it's the stuff that doesn't fit that we learn the most from.

As my adventures in London and Amsterdam showed, once our minds get convinced about something, we often are no longer able to see the things that no longer fit our beliefs. Perversely enough, our strong beliefs rob us of the perceptions and experiences which could shake up our beliefs.

The curious reader may point out that the idea that all beliefs are limiting is also a belief. Sure, and while all beliefs are limiting in the sense that they dispose us to pay attention to some aspects at the expense of others, all beliefs aren't necessarily equally limiting.

Grinder has often made the point that you can act as if you believe something to see what the consequences are of operating out of that filter in some context. I agree, and find much wisdom in his suggestion that many concepts and formats can be useful to the agent of change until you start believing in them. At the same time, there are probably also some advantages that go with the costly beliefs of the true believer.

How does this apply to judges likely getting worse at evaluation and decision making after decades of experience? A lot is the short answer. Remember that beliefs tend to be self-reinforcing. We unconsciously organize our lives to reinforce our beliefs without realizing that we are doing it.

Consider how people often socialize with people who mostly share their values and beliefs, how the literature we read and news and talk shows we watch are mostly in alignment with our political beliefs. Internal factors such as confirmation bias and external factors like media, peer group and the implicit assumptions inherent in our profession contribute to our tunnel vision.

A judge has received a long formal education. Formal education is a heavy indoctrination process into a belief system and has a tendency to reward successful indoctrination, evidenced by conformity and making the deeper assumptions part of one's identity. Curiosity and questioning of sacred beliefs, premises and assumptions are seldom rewarded in any hierarchical power structure. The amount of orthodoxy and conformity in professions such as medicine, psychology and law is mind blowing.

Judges have, along with psychiatrists, a lot of power—way more than medical doctors and psychologists. Power has a tendency to reduce perspective-taking. Those with a lot of power and social status are disposed to stick to their own perspective and by definition don't have to adapt much. It's often the underdog who has to learn more about how others see the world in order to effectively persuade.

In the Norwegian justice system, judges have a lot of power but zero personal responsibility for exercising that power with wisdom. As far as I am aware, no judge has ever had to face any personal consequence for convicting the innocent. This also applies in cases where they have demonstrably *not* exercised good judgment nor anything near the impartiality they are supposed to have.

Add to this the absence of a feedback system that could lead to course correction. In the Norwegian legal system there is no documentation of what happens (no audio/video recording or stenography) in the majority of court cases.

A surgeon whose patient dies on the operating table receives direct feedback. The engineer whose bridge collapses receives direct feedback. The judge who sends an innocent person to jail will most likely never find out. The system is designed to protect those with power, not the principles of justice. Add to the lack of documentation something referred to as "evidence-free evaluation" which essentially says that even if no evidence holds up, the judge is supposed to come to a conclusion based on an "overall evaluation". In actuality, this means that if the judge feels you are guilty, he is free to call that *evidence* that you are guilty beyond reasonable doubt.

What happens when judges, under these conditions, have no insight into the structure of subjective experiences? When topics like the reconstructive nature of memory, cognitive dissonance and confirmation bias aren't even part of their education? Here you have a culture and a system that reinforces the judges' confirmation bias and protects them from discovering their screw-ups.

Imagine a typical judge who believes that he reaches his conclusions through objective analysis and reason, who believes in his profession and the legal system, *and* who sincerely believes that his decades of experience have made him an expert on detecting lies and truthfulness. Besides, they're probably all guilty, otherwise they wouldn't have been charged.

I forgot to tell you that the prosecution and the police share the same bed in Norway. The prosecution orders the actual police investigation. It should be pretty obvious that this is a recipe for disaster. In fact, in several cases of convicting the innocent, the jury has realized the person's innocence and wanted to acquit. However, the judges have been convinced of the innocent person's guilt.

It's very likely that judges decide quickly, then use

reasoning and legal knowledge to justify the decision. The availability bias (how easily similar guilty convictions come to mind) combined with confirmation bias and "listening along well-known tracks" provides the basis for strong internal coherence, resulting in a certain feeling that the person is guilty whether or not he is.

The Norwegian media has a part to play in this as well. The large newspapers are partly sponsored by the state and loyal to establishment power structures. In the cases of convicting the innocent that have later been reversed due to activists' and private investigators' efforts, the Norwegian media has been on the side of police and prosecution from day one, often mocking those working tirelessly on behalf of the defendants. Then, once the cat is out of the bag (often decades later) the media is remarkably silent.

Many psychologists reacted with shock and disbelief when Robin Dawes released *House Of Cards*, the explosive book that showed overwhelming evidence that there is no correlation at all between having a psychology degree and being an effective psychotherapist, that psychologists are no better than psychotherapists without formal qualifications, and just as shockingly, that decades of experience lead to no improvement whatsoever. And, as previously mentioned, their capacity for detecting lies, guilt and future crime are no better than that of the average person. Of course knowing this doesn't stop them from acting as if and presenting themselves as having these capacities in a court of law.

But is there really much reason to be that surprised? Imagine a tennis player or entrepreneur who had to spend year after year in school learning various theories without developing any of the attributes necessary for the real time demands. Imagine studying tennis history and strategy for many years. Then after all those years (hardly ever holding a racquet) you then have to start playing real tournaments.

Chances are your theories are going to get in the way. Instead of learning based on direct experience, you will likely attempt to fit experience into your learned theories and beliefs. Likewise, there isn't much in psychology education to help you develop the attributes relevant for high-quality change work—the ability to develop the rapport, to calibrate responses, to evoke responses, to think strategically, to confront and challenge, to have strong boundaries and a capacity for courage and compassion, etc.

"Oh, come on, the members of these professions are very intelligent", some may protest. The implication being that those with above-average brain power, as defined by IQ tests, are too rational and logical to be acting as stupidly as I claim. While I would personally challenge this concept of intelligence as way too narrow, let's assume that IQ testing measures general intelligence, and that the members of these status professions, especially those who do well, are highly intelligent.

This may be a part of the problem. First of all, those who perceive themselves (and are perceived so by others) as intelligent and who identify with that, will often only be willing to learn from those higher up in whatever hierarchy they belong to.

This of course ensures that there are few people they may be willing to listen to. In fact, the smarter they or other people think they are, the fewer people they're willing to listen to. Furthermore, screwing up, making mistakes or looking stupid will often be very scary to those whose identity is that of a very intelligent person.

Michael Shermer, in his book *Why People Believe Weird Things*, devotes a chapter to the topic of why very intelligent people often believe weird things. Shermer's answer is that smart people believe in weird/stupid stuff because they are skilled at using their reasoning skills to defend beliefs they arrived at for non-smart reasons.

Going back to the brain as a "belief engine", our brains create patterns and project agenticity, and do so without what we call intelligence having much to do with it. That cherished ability to use logic and reason primarily comes into play when defending, explaining and arguing for our beliefs. This explains how the highly intelligent can have a harder time getting themselves out of wacky belief systems.

Shermer cites some studies on this topic in the book I just mentioned. The research suggests that the highly intelligent are simultaneously much better at defending their beliefs *and* poorer at considering alternative explanations. If you want to turn these folks into a menace to society, give them plenty of power so as to reduce their perspective-taking tendencies even more. Indoctrinate them into a belief system and make sure they never get any direct real-world experience. Delude them into thinking they make decisions using reason and logic. Make sure not to hold them accountable for their screwups and make sure there is no documentation or feedback system. Give them a robe, call them judges, and you have a recipe for...stupidity. Give them a few decades and they will get more and more stupid while thinking they are getting wiser and wiser.

Sounds like the highly intelligent design of systemic stupidity.

WE SUCK TOO

The *we* I'm referring to here are primarily those with a background in NLP and hypnosis. The NLP and hypnosis worlds are also largely organized in a way that serves to reinforce our beliefs instead of challenging and updating them.

One of the worst ideas ever is the master practitioner title in NLP. Some people are certified as NLP practitioners after one week of training. Those who certify that way also usually certify people as master practitioners after an additional two weeks. A master practitioner after 21 days of training.

This is a joke, and a bad one to boot.

Imagine someone calling themselves a master gymnast after 21 days of training. Anyone not indoctrinated or consumed by greed can see how fraudulent it is to call anyone a master of anything in 21 days. How about master martial artist, violinist or mathematician?

In many cases, if you invest an additional three weeks of training you can be an NLP trainer.

Six weeks of training and you are encouraged, as I was, to start your own training company and certify NLP practitioners and master practitioners—no competency or real-world experience needed! This is not a field with respect for itself or its students, nor do I believe that those who certify in this way love this profession.

If you have any knowledge of the NLP training world, you will realize that I just called the vast majority of NLP trainers frauds. This is exactly what I'm saying and I stand by it! I have been pointing out this stuff for a long time, and it's not a popularly received message. We are training and certifying incompetent idiots and labeling as masters those who are actually just beginners.

Common sense suggests that people who get these certificates realize that they are incompetent beginners. Common sense is often wrong, and it's usually wrong here as well.

People invest a lot of money in NLP training. Then, once they get certified, cognitive dissonance kicks in. On the one hand people may know they are far from masters. On the other hand they are being certified as masters by seemingly competent experts, and will often rationalize that they wouldn't have gotten certified if they weren't competent. They have to justify their investment of time and money. Besides, some trickery and deception is often added to the mix. Often they have been told that there is no need to worry, they have "gotten it all unconsciously". Yup...it's been unconsciously installed. Sheer nonsense, but attractive. The fact that NLP techniques often can provide rapid change and dramatic demos help make plausible the idea that they can somehow master NLP quicker than anything else.

Remember, the feeling of certainty is primarily due to coherence. It's easy to get internal coherence when there are just a few pieces in the mental puzzle. The feeling of understanding gets confused with actual competency. The less someone knows about something the less they usually think there is to know. So, with good help from internal coherence, cognitive dissonance and confirmation bias, we get certified master practitioners with much certainty and little skill. The emphasis on feeling good, changing beliefs and changing your state to access an all-knowing unconscious mind also helps.

When you add to this a culture that inspires them to launch their own training company even if they have to rely

189

on others' stories to make money fast, then there is no wonder how hyped-up this field has gotten.

These newbie masters can't compete unless they do it through hype.

The hypnosis world is even worse. While many hypnosis instructors have actually seen some clients, compared to the armchair generals of the NLP world, the industry "standards" are horrible. It's quite common for people to be certified as professional (or master...ugh) hypnotists after seven days of training. Some certify their students after a weekend course. Heck, some will certify you if you buy some DVDs from a weekend course.

The consequences are ugly. Black and white thinking power hypnotists, with certainty and belief after a weekend course, convinced that a trance induction and some direct suggestions from a script is all it takes. These guys have no idea of all the relevant stuff they *don't* know, and since they hardly know anything, they think there is hardly anything to know.

Their instructors will usually claim in marketing that they succeed all the time and have one format for all issues at all times.

Those who do seven-day courses may even encourage their students to go out and do hypnotic regression work and parts therapy without practice time or even demonstrating the techniques in class. The repressed memory versus false memory craze of the eighties and nineties isn't even mentioned, nor anything from memory research. Modern cognitive and social psychology is usually ignored, but old Freudian concepts combined with new-age drivel such as past lives, entity work and sometimes even alien abduction work, rule the day.

I have to admit the alien stuff is rare, though.

As someone who is passionate and cares about the profession, it's frustrating to watch it in many ways becoming anti-science, anti-reason and pro-new-age babble.

Unfortunately, many students end up on forums with other true believers and many live happily ever after with their flawed notions protected by confirmation bias and group thinking.

Still, as tragic as this is, the solution is not more government regulation; academics seldom make great agents of change. Pit a group of psychologists against an NLP master practitioner group with 21 days of training and a little experience, and the NLP group will win. Sad, but most likely true. Those who have a week of training in hypnotic age regression and some experience will likely beat both groups as long as mid-range hypnotic capacity is present.

That's what I suspect after 16 years of full-time change work.

It's important for those of us who work with hypnosis to be extra mindful of the topic of expectations. Daniel Wegner makes some excellent points in his book *The Illusion of Conscious Will*. He calls hypnosis a "nightmare science" and refers to it as "the thing that changes into what you think it is". The suggestibility of hypnotized clients is a key point in them "performing" as suggested. Wegner says, "The effect of suggestions passes not only from hypnotist to subject, but from subject to hypnotist. One patient with remarkable symptoms can create beliefs in the hypnotist about the forms that hypnotic manifestations will take. These can then be transmitted unwittingly as suggestions to other patients, who then act to confirm the hypnotist's expectations. An epidemic of standard responses to hypnosis results. The circle of influence can also promote a kind of social memory. Previous performances by the subject are recalled by the hypnotist and suggested again, then to be performed again by the subject. Thus, the hypnotist develops the conviction that there is a pattern in the subject's behavior when none would have arisen otherwise. It's easy to see how the hypnotist's theory of the thing changes the thing which then changes the hypnotist's theory."

I couldn't agree more with Wegner and he said it better than I could.

DEBRIEFING DEBUNKED

Some people have gotten quite irritated and called me an overcomplicator when raising concerns around expectations and self-reinforcing feedback loops. These folks claim that things are a lot simpler than I make them out to be and that all one has to do is to use some common sense. Besides, they get feedback from clients and know what kind of results they are getting.

Debriefing seems to some like common sense. It's mandatory in many countries for medical, military and law enforcement personnel to go through debriefing within 72 hours of some potentially traumatizing event. Here the person "empties" himself by verbally describing what happened in detail so they can "get it out of their system". Common sense says that it's a great idea. Experienced professionals who have massive experience conducting it rave about it. After all, they know it works because they see the results. Besides, patients rave about it and tell the experts that it has really helped them. Quite simple, right?

Not so fast. The meta-studies are in and they clearly show that debriefing doesn't work. It gets worse—not only does it not work, but it's counterproductive. Compared to control groups, those in debriefing groups are much worse off when it comes to developing typical post-trauma symptoms.

I don't have any fantastic solution. Change work will always be an art and had better be informed by scientific findings and the scientific method.

193

An important question to ask yourself is, "To what extent have I organized my professional life in a way that protects and reinforces my beliefs? And to what extent have I created an environment for myself conducive to challenging my own beliefs and assumptions as well as those of my peers?"

How many sources do you learn from? How solid and wide is your feedback system?

Do you have good bartenders and receptionists in your life who can alert you to your own nuttiness, and are you willing to be "bartendered" by people whom you may both dislike and strongly disagree with?

MIND ABSOLUTISM

Camilla was furious and deeply offended when she stormed out of the hospital and swore she would never go back. She had been living with a rather aggressive breast cancer for a while, and the oncologist was struggling to convince Camilla that she needed surgery to save her life. Camilla's belief system prevented his message from being heard and the doctor ended up calling her an idiot and ridiculing her beliefs.

Camilla had some NLP training. She was also a "new-ager" convinced that the mind held the key to curing disease.

She called me, told her story, and asked for my help. I agreed to help with the intent of helping her to eliminate the cancer. While I was more than willing to help on her terms, I simultaneously had a different goal on her behalf. This may sound arrogant and even unethical to some NLP purists, where imposing content on the client is akin to swearing in church.

My goal was to develop good enough rapport with her so that I could persuade her to go back to the hospital and have the surgery if need be. While I do my best to respect people's right to choose, stupidity is stupidity, whether it's my own bullshit or anyone else's.

If I developed, say, testicular cancer, where western medicine has a very high success rate, it would have been stupid of me to decline treatment. Make no mistake, I would still explore my own internal world and relationship, but it can be done simultaneously. This is about pragmatism and reason.

Cases like these are cases where I'm OK with imposing my own values and beliefs.

Camilla was not a very good hypnotic subject, but we made the best of what we had. We worked with traumatic memories, resolved some inner conflicts, worked on establishing better boundaries, more self- and other-acceptance and better relationship to her own thoughts and feelings.

She made some huge shifts internally and gained a lot from our work together. She later told me that she had wanted to kill herself, and had decided to do so if I couldn't help her.

The work we did together did not cure her cancer or reduce it. However, tests at the hospital, about six months after we started work together, showed that the tumor had not increased at all, which surprised the doctors, given how aggressive it was. Perhaps our work had something to do with that, but then again maybe not.

My goal was a success, though. She went back to her doctor and had a successful surgery. When we last spoke a year or so later she was still free of cancer. Oh, and she was very happy for my content imposition and said that she would have never done the surgery had it not been for the work we did together.

By all means, do your best to impose as little content as possible, and at the same time, be pragmatic enough that you don't end up with a dead client when you can save a life by "swearing in church". And push NLP patterning and hypnosis to the max while simultaneously realizing that these interventions may range in effectiveness between complete resolutions of some disease, to effective pain management, to coping better with a disease to no effectiveness at all. Sometimes surgery, drugs and changes in diet will be a lot more relevant. Don't end up in either/or camp. Adopt a both/and perspective.

Unfortunately, medical doctors often completely ignore subjective and inter-subjective factors when working with patients, and contribute to much unnecessary suffering and pain.

Seven or eight years ago I worked with a very hard-core skeptic who was also a nurse. A smoker for 38 years, she was smoking between 40-50 cigarettes a day and had never even lasted one day when she had previously attempted to quit smoking. She had zero belief in hypnosis and later told me that she had come to see me to get her husband off her back. She needed throat surgery, and her doctors had been on her case for years to get her to stop smoking. I don't know why, but they could not do the surgery as long as she smoked.

She was an excellent hypnotic subject and came out of hypnosis completely done with smoking. She later told me that it was as if she had never smoked and was never tempted nor did she have any stress or withdrawal symptoms at all.

A year later a health magazine published her story, and she went ahead and finally had the surgery.

The sad part is that while some of the doctors were pleased that hypnosis worked, none of them ever called me or sent me a patient. Scientifically-minded doctors can be as stuck as "new-agers" when a solution doesn't quite fit their belief system.

GET RAPED—FEEL BETTER

Elizabeth reported that her anxiety was virtually gone since our first session together about ten days earlier. But it wasn't so much what happened in the office that had reduced her anxiety; it was that she had gotten raped.

To most people, the idea that rape would cause someone to release anxiety and feel relief and confidence probably sounds unbelievable, but Elizabeth had struggled with severe anxiety and compulsive thinking for years. She was also a big believer in the philosophy that has been popularized by the book and movie called *The Secret*. The so-called secret is the alleged law of attraction. Whatever you focus on you attract by the "law" of attraction. So, if you get raped you created that with your mind and attracted the rapist with your thoughts.

Now, since she had thought about a lot of nasty stuff, including rape, to her that meant that "it finally happened". She had "known" that something really bad was going to happen for a long time, and when it finally did it meant that she was right. Besides, it proved how powerful her mind was and that she was in control. With a belief system like that, it's possible to feel better after being raped.

Some mind absolutists and new-agers might applaud this change in Elizabeth. Some NLP purists of the "never impose content school" might personally disagree with her belief system, but leave it alone.

I decided to pick her new-age babble apart. She was

extremely uncomfortable and anxious during the process.

I pointed out to her that she didn't actually know that something bad would happen. She had *thought* that something bad would happen and something bad had happened, but that does not mean that there is any correlation between the two. She was tasked with writing assignments where she compared the many catastrophic thoughts she had had and how many of them had turned out to happen.

I gave her the symptom prescription task of imagining all sorts of horrible stuff and to write down the actual outcomes. The purpose was mainly to help her dispute the idea that she needed to be in control of her thoughts and her life, and to deal better with ambiguity. She came to realize how little "control" she had and to deal better with that. That's a long-term solution for anxiety that actually works. To dispute musturbation, learn to treat thoughts as thoughts and to accept the uncertainties and ambiguities of life, and to learn useful skills for the future.

Elizabeth had gotten drunk at a party, passed out on a bed, and awoke to being raped by a guy who had given her creepy vibes earlier that night.

She was tasked with taking up realistic self-defense training to get more street smart. This way the next time she got a creepy vibe from some guy she would not continue drinking in his presence and delude herself into thinking that she can behave however she wants, and be safe, as long as she projects Prince Charming in her mind.

While having goals and imagining reaching them can be useful, as long as you are willing to act as well, there is no law of attraction. It's utter bullshit, even if attractive to many fearful folks because it gives them the illusion of control.

Think about the implications of The Secret. It would mean, if true, that the kids who are being killed in Syria at the time of this writing have attracted their murderers through their thoughts. That's how ridiculous it is. How can I be sure that it is nonsense? Well, I have gotten clients to deliberately imagine planes crashing, and with hundreds of fear of flying clients none of them have been able to make a plane crash with their thoughts.

Come to think of it, if this law of attraction stuff was true, then obsessive stalkers would end up in bed with the Hollywood star of their wet dreams, rather than in a cell having to be the wife of some big bearded guy with a pot belly. Fantasizing about Angelina Jolie but getting Don Desperate in a prison cell might be a more likely outcome for the obsessed stalker.

IS PERCEPTION PROJECTION?

In his book *The Inside Out Revolution* (great book), Michael Neill writes the following: "You're in an art studio filled with painters standing at their easels. Although you can't see it from where you're standing, they're all looking in the direction of a small platform in the center of the room and painting what they see. As you walk around the studio, you notice small and sometimes vast discrepancies between what people are painting on their canvases. Arguments break out, in part of the room, as to whether or not the model for the painting is more one color than another, taller or shorter, uglier or more beautiful than rendered.

"You begin to be curious about what it is that everyone is painting, so you make your way to the center of the room and discover to your surprise that there is absolutely nothing there. The emptiness of the center is palpable.

"Suddenly, you realize the reason why everyone's painting a different picture isn't down to their point of view, where their easel happens to be placed, or even to a matter of personal interpretation. It's because what they are 'viewing' is only a projection of their own thoughts!"

Neill's writing is based on the teachings of Sydney Banks. Banks had an enlightenment experience where he realized that we live in a world of thought, a world that is actually created from thought. This way of understanding our experience

201

is one that is inside out, as opposed to the common outside in.

Banks and his students claim that we don't experience our children, parents or partners, but rather our thinking about our children, parents and partners. In other words, what I see is all made up and I live in a world of thought.

Sydney Banks isn't the only one with an enlightenment experience whose teachings have made an impact in the coaching and psychotherapy world.

Byron Katie's approach called The Work seems very similar. Katie also had an enlightenment experience that she refers to as "waking up to reality". Katie, in her book *A Thousand Names for Joy*, says, "I discovered that when I believed my thoughts I suffered, but then when I didn't believe them I didn't suffer, and that is true for every human being. I found that suffering is optional. I found joy within me that has never disappeared, not for a single moment. That joy is in everyone, always."

Katie claims that the material world is a metaphor for mind.

While I have enjoyed reading about their work and have applied their teachings, I do think that people like Byron Katie and Sydney Banks go too far in claiming that perception is exclusively projection. I have little doubt that projection is a significant aspect of perception. My hotel adventures in London and Amsterdam illustrate this beautifully. Here I projected stories of irresponsible receptionists and dishonest waiters, then responded to those projections as if they were the other person. Then I projected helpful receptionists and professional waiters and attributed those qualities to the other person. As Banks would say, I was feeling my thoughts about the other person. To me, they were my story about who they were.

However, perception is also partly detection. When I work

with a client who experiences fear, I can detect fear from his or her micro-muscle facial expression without feeling any fear myself. Even in my hotel adventures I could eventually detect what time it was according to consensus reality and being able to detect that changed my projections.

I think that while the common outside-in view gives rise to victimhood, the inside-out view is an overreaction. My hunch is that a *betweenness* position is more accurate.

Iain McGilchrist offers some beautiful examples of this, in one of my favorite books, *The Master and his Emissary*.

Consider viewing a mountain. You could say that the experience of a mountain is a betweeness phenomenon; it comes into being when whatever is out there and the human nervous system interact. It's a combined detection and projection. For example, the colors we think we see out there are created by our brains and projected out there. We also project the value and meaning of mountain whether that's being a sacred place, a rock climbers' Mecca or a profit machine during tourist season. But there is something out there and you can project whatever you want, but you will still hurt yourself if you run head first into the mountain or dive from the top without a parachute.

The sense of an "I" also comes into being simultaneously with the mountain as the sense of an "I" is dependent upon something projected as "other" to be recreated moment by moment.

So while you can say that the world is a projection of thought, thought is also a projection of the world.

The term "mind" is somewhat problematic. Banks uses "mind" as a label for the intelligence we are all part of, the energy and intelligence that ensures that babies grow teeth and cuts heal. Others may imply an entity that creates thoughts and imply that this mental activity is somehow separate from the physical body. The term "minding" may be more appropriate here, as I am referring to thinking, projecting, meaning-making, etc.—processes that are physiological and not some mind-body split. At the same time I'm open to using the term in much the same way as Sydney Banks is using it.

To say that our thoughts create our world seems very one-sided and had better be complemented with acknowledging that the world creates our thoughts. Your social-political-economic living conditions have a strong influence on what appears as thoughts. If you lived in an isolated tribal society, the idea of checking your e-mail would never occur to you. Our culture and language automatically influences and tweaks thoughts before they reach conscious awareness. Consider how our language is disposing us to think in terms of "to be" and the "is of identity" primes us to think in either/or terms. Those who learn E-Prime and replace "is" with "seems" open up a more both/and thinking style.

Social psychology has clearly established that we behave differently with just one other person in the room. We are influenced whether we want to be or not. Daniel Kahneman points out how crucial framing can be in influencing our decision-making. In countries where the socio-economic conditions are very similar there are huge differences in how willing people are to donate their organs. In Sweden 86% are willing while in Denmark only 4% are willing. It turns out that framing is the difference that makes the difference.

In Sweden the government sends out a form that takes for granted that you will donate your organs. To decline, you have to mark out a "no" and return the form. It takes more effort to decline than to comply. In Denmark it's the other way around.

There have been studies that show that feelings of disgust, triggered by a dirty cinema or a foul smell, influence participants to judge more harshly the immoral acts they see on the screen. This finding shows that our feelings may be unconsciously influenced by factors in our environment.

We can apply this to hypnosis and change work as well. A few cling to an outside-in view where the hypnotist makes the subject change. Here the hypnotist's intent, congruence and skills are where it's at. Some "power hypnotists" think they can hypnotize anyone, while others may think that they are the ones who create the hypnosis, but that the client needs the "neurological architecture" for it to happen.

Others claim that all hypnosis is self-hypnosis. Here the guide is less important, and it's the client who is credited with making the change.

Once again, I think that hypnosis and change work is more accurately described as a *betweenness* phenomenon. The hypnotist and his skills and action matter and so do the abilities, skills and engagement of the client. The framing and relationship factors matter a lot as well.

One of my first NLP instructors, a guy by the name of Tad James, seems to be a mind absolutist. He teaches cause = effect and directly states, much like those who teach The Secret, that we create everything that happens to us. In other words, if you were a Jewish child who got killed by the Nazis, you created that with your mind. If you are a passenger on a plane that crashes, then that too, is supposedly the result of a conscious or unconscious limiting decision.

I should point out that this new-age babble has nothing to do with NLP, and it's nothing that Grinder, Bandler or Pucelik have endorsed. Plenty of NLP trainers teach it though, since James has certified so many trainers.

Tad James also teaches that "there is no-one out there"— the world is a projection of your mind.

While James acknowledges that these ideas may not necessarily be true, he claims that it's useful to act as if they are.

I remember with amusement being an assistant at James's

trainers training almost fifteen years ago. In the morning, be-fore the attendees would arrive, Tad met the assistants for a little pep talk. He started out telling stories to evoke guilt and fear. One story was about a worker in a moving company who had found a dollar on the floor in a home. He had debat-ed with himself whether to give his boss the dollar. When he chose to give the dollar to his boss, the boss had said that it was good that he did, since he would have had to fire him if he hadn't.

The next story was about how Tad's mother had died during a training of his and how he couldn't go to the funeral because he had a job to do and how he expected that level of commitment from everyone! Keep in mind that the assistants were unpaid volunteers.

The stories kept coming for an hour or so.

Later, when the new participants arrived, he was all "sweet and gentle" and told them that they "were the light".

He started the training session really hammering in the cause = effect and perception is projection frames.

To the extent that participants buy into Tad's framing, they buy into the idea that everything they see in him is ex-clusively a projection of their own mind. If Tad behaves un-ethically or anyone's bullshit detector goes off, it just means that it is time to do more work on your own unresolved stuff, until all you see in Tad is love and light. Of course, Tad has courses, which he enthusiastically sells from the platform, designed to help you clean up your projections.

During his attempts to sell further courses he would use stage anchoring to attempt to link strong feelings of guilt and fear to any objection the participants may have had to-wards attending. Normally the "creepy vibe" many reported might have been interpreted as a sign to keep one's eyes and ears open and to do some investigation. Here, for those who bought into the frame, the "creepy vibe" was an invitation to do work on oneself until Tad was all sweet and light irrespective of how he behaved.

During the course Tad claimed to have discovered and invented aspects of NLP that others pioneered. He used stage anchoring to link people's deepest fears and guilt to any objection to attending his future courses, and he had just taken the domain names of RichardBandler.com and JohnGrinder.com so that anyone clicking on those would get redirected to Tad's site.

He talked a lot about integrity and ethics so I confronted him about the websites. First he blamed his son and said they did it to protect the names so that, say, John Grinder, the barber in Arizona, wouldn't take it. When I stated that I didn't believe him, he exploded: "In business, it's use it or lose it, motherfucker!" This I could believe. While quite a few liked that I stirred things up, many were uncomfortable and didn't want to rock the boat, although they were happy to gossip about it in private.

My observation was that many of those who had bought into Tad's framing were conformist sheeple who went along exclaiming "Wonderful! Perfect! That's Great!" no matter what happened, since doing so meant that they were deeply spiritually evolved since they only projected love and light.

The Catholic Church has tried this strategy with their pedophile child-molesting priests. Pretending that the priests are clean and loving doesn't change the brutal facts regarding child molestation and massive cover-ups.

The mind absolutists will claim that hurtful feelings are a sign that your thinking is all crooked. However, you may have spotted/detected something where the "bad" feelings may be useful. There is some research showing that those who have engaged in depression are often more accurate in assessing others' views about them. And, sometimes happiness may contribute to us being rather superficial in our thinking, and so-called negative feelings may be useful in helping develop more accurate observations.

My current thinking is that perception is both detection *and* projection, and that our experience is created from between.

Therefore I recommend a both/and approach. In the case of Tad James I do find many of his practices, claims and actions unethical. At the same time I do think that to the extent that I get emotional thinking about it (which I no longer do) I have some shadow work to do. When I angered myself by thinking, "Tad is fucking dishonest", I knew it was time to do a turnaround.

The turnaround "my thinking is dishonest" allowed me to see that to insist that Tad should be honest, when he clearly isn't, is dishonest thinking on my part. By acknowledging and owning my own dishonesty I can see our common humanity.

These turnarounds, which Byron Katie teaches, have been golden to me, and I have done them so much that they're alive inside of me.

Just the other day I lost my temper a bit when dealing with a super-bureaucrat unable to think for himself or exercise any personal responsibility. While I think my assessment of him is probably very accurate in that his way of thinking is rigid, that he doesn't really think for himself, and that he takes little personal responsibility, I was—well, a few minutes later, after calling him a lobotomized idiot—able to find those qualities internally by doing some turnarounds.

I turned it around to, "My thinking is rigid." It didn't take long to see that I was doing some rigid thinking at that moment. I have a tendency, sometimes, to demand that people be pragmatic and truth-seeking and that they think for themselves, but these are *my* preferences, not theirs. Clearly, he shouldn't think by himself until he does, anymore than it should stop snowing outside until it does.

The turnaround "he shouldn't exercise personal responsibility" also seems more accurate. He shouldn't until he does.

Another turnaround was, "*I* should exercise personal responsibility and think for myself."

I blamed him for pissing me off instead of acknowledging my own shouldn't-ing. And maybe it was time to think for myself and challenge whether it's necessarily true that people should think for themselves.

As soon as the turnarounds went to work internally, I once again found my sense of humor. To be a great agent of change I think you will have to both be able to read people pretty accurately while simultaneously being alert to your own projections. It's a both/and game. Your projections and expectations will influence your clients, but they are not the only games in town.

I remember vividly working with two female smokers in the same week a few years ago. One smoker seemed committed, seemed to respond wonderfully and was a fantastic hypnotic subject. I fully expected her to stop smoking. The second smoker was the complete opposite and I couldn't evoke a single hypnotic phenomenon.

I gave up and told her I couldn't help her and gave her money back. Since she struggled with chronic fatigue syndrome I recommended she read *The Divided Mind* by Dr. John Sarno. I didn't expect her to follow through.

Five weeks later, to my genuine surprise, she called and said that she hadn't even thought about smoking since that day at my office. And she had almost completely let go of chronic fatigue syndrome by reading John Sarno's book.

My excellent hypnotic subject came in twice and lasted a few hours each time before she started smoking again. After the second session she gave up and I gave her half her money back.

Prepare to be humbled and for your clients to mess with your projections and expectations, and be grateful. By the way, if you have become something of a mind absolutist, then I recommend you check out Spiral Dynamics. While I have some disagreements with the model, it really helped me gain an appreciation for the interplay between living conditions and meaning-making systems. Ken Wilber's integral approach, especially his four-quadrant model will also help stretch your thinking.

GOING DEVELOPMENTAL
(AND SWEARING IN CHURCH)

It can often be very challenging—even dangerous—to work as the lone bouncer at a bar full of "shady characters". If you tend to the people at the door, and you don't have a partner inside, conflict can escalate into violence before you are able to intervene.

One Friday night I saw two guys arguing, each backed by several loyal supporters. All the pre-contact cues were present to indicate that one guy was about to sucker punch the other. Thankfully, I was able to intervene just in time to prevent a tag-team bar brawl.

"He drove past me!" Those were the exact words from the seemingly most aggressive one. I was completely baffled by this complaint and replied by pointing out that a number of people drive past him every time he parks his car in public. Both of them were genuinely baffled by my sincere comment. It was as if they could see that I just didn't get it while simultaneously not understanding how I could not "get" what was so obvious to both of them.

This unintended mutual confusion helped defuse the situation enough that we could talk without anyone looking like he was setting the other guy up for a sucker punch.

In the somewhat heated verbal exchange between the two of them I "got" that "drive by" meant "disrespect", and that the solution seemed to be either one guy backing down or a violent exchange to "get respect".

211

Neither man backed down, so since violence seemed to be the next step, I offered a different solution—a solution in the form of a challenge that would be hard to decline since doing so would equal losing face and respect.

I framed it by asking both of them if they were man enough to accept a challenge. They were to get in their respective cars and race each other three circuits around the city center. The loser would have to buy the winner a beer.

While highly irresponsible, it seemed to be a functional trade off. They both stepped up to the plate, the loser bought a beer for the winner, and no-one got hurt in the race or in the bar.

Working as a bouncer in a bar right after six weeks of NLP training in California offered quite a contrast—a contrast that I suspect may have "planted a seed" that later culminated in adult developmental psychology resonating deeply with me.

The clientele at the bar seemed almost like a different breed of people, even when sober, than those I met during NLP training. You may say of course they're different—first of all a bar is a very different context than a seminar, and alcohol is a key factor. I agree.

However a couple of years down the road, I was hired to work as a consultant with the long-term unemployed, acting as a combination of motivational speaker, coach and psychotherapist. Here I got to fine tune my skills at provocation artistry and I share generously from this period in my book *Provocative Hypnosis*.

The folks I met here seemed, as a group, very different from many of those I saw in my private practice. I also got the same vibe from them as I'd gotten from those at the bar, despite sobriety and a change of context. They seemed like sober versions of the characters at the bar.

Fast-forward another thirteen years: These days I have many conversations with members of the prison population.

These men and women also offer a distinct contrast from my regular clients in private practice. At this point you are probably not surprised to hear that I find the persons in prison remarkably similar to both the bar folks and the long-term unemployed seminar participants.

During my NLP training, even though personality typologies like the Myers-Briggs Type Indicator (MBTI) are not part of NLP, we spent quite a bit of time on Myers-Briggs, and I found it interesting. However, a tool like Myers-Briggs didn't offer much in helping me understand the difference between the groups. Clearly, people at the bar and at the NLP training had different personality temperaments compared to members of their own "tribe". For those of you familiar with the five-factor model, I can say that the bar group, long term unemployed and prison population would score lower on traits such as conscientiousness and agreeableness. No big surprise there.

While the persons in prison (and the other groups) have different personalities and vary in their intelligence, a large percentage of them seem to share some tendencies, one of which is a short time horizon with little regard for future consequences—the future is the present that hasn't happened yet. Another is an exclusive focus on the physical world and a concrete black-and-white thinking style with little, if any, self-reflection. Their relationships are exploitative, and others are of interest to the extent that they can be "suppliers to the self". Might is right and whatever you can get away with is legitimate. They share an absence of inner standards or ideology and a lack of concern with idealism or devotion to a larger cause. Their sense of humor is often hostile, their trust level is low, blame is externalized ("it's not my fault"), and if they end up in trouble it's due to hanging out with the wrong crowd.

I know, I know, I just described your teenage son, the

one who might have traded you in for a six-pack and some cigarettes on a warm summer day. While the mindset I just described may be most commonly associated with imperial youth—an attitude of others being seen as suppliers to the self—research shows that quite a few adults operate here as well.

Let me be very clear. I am *not* suggesting that all the people in the above-mentioned groups have this mindset. What I am suggesting is that you will find this form of mind overrepresented among the characters in prison and in "rough" bars.

Looking back, the NLP folks I spent time with in California and my private clients, for all their differences, seem to have very different tendencies from the groups mentioned above: Many have long-term goals they're working to achieve. They are in varying degrees more psychologically-oriented; they reflect on their thinking. Many experience themselves as authoring their own experiences and don't hold others responsible for how they feel. Neither do they think they cause others' emotional states.

Some are highly devoted to a cause or some ideology, and many are in mutually rewarding relationships or are looking to have such relationships.

THE SELF-SOVEREIGN MIND

Those of you familiar with adult developmental psychology are, just like NLP and hypnosis folks, aware that we humans actively make meaning out of experience. So far, so good. Those coming at this from a developmental angle believe that when adults (not just children) grow and evolve over time, they do so in rather predictable ways—that they enter qualitatively different phases as they evolve.

Those who are familiar with the work of Clare Graves and the Spiral Dynamics System founded by Chris Cowan and Don Beck will recognize my bar/prison description as a typical C-P system or red ᵛMEME (meaning-making system) at work.

If you have studied Ego Development with Jane Loevinger or Susanne Cook-Greuter, then you will recognize my description as one describing the opportunist's way of understanding himself and the world.

In Robert Kegan's model, the description I offered fits his second order of consciousness or Self-Sovereign Mind.

While I have learned a lot from both Chris Cowan about Gravesian System/Spiral Dynamics, and Susanne Cook-Greuter about Ego Development, I prefer and find most useful Robert Kegan's model for the type of work that I do.

I feel compelled to offer a couple of warnings as we approach the topic of meaning-making systems and their application to change work. First off, it's complicated stuff. I have been studying these models intensely for about seven years and still think I only have a basic understanding of them.

A model like this, while concerned with the structure of subjective experience, is still content imposition. Viewing another person through the lens of a model may result in fitting the person to match the model as well as projecting onto the person the stuff that doesn't fit. We may even be doing this at the expense of picking up relevant stuff from the client due to confirmation bias.

At the same time I do think that the benefit of having a model like this outweighs the risks. It's helped me to gain better rapport and responsiveness since it enabled me to better tailor interventions that, to quote Kegan, firmly anchor a bridge on each side. In the case of people transitioning between two systems, the model makes it easier to "speak" to both systems and thereby foster deeper and more ecological change. The model has also given me a useful road map in terms of what the client likely can't see as well as what he is likely moving towards in terms of how he structures his experience. Furthermore, having a functional road map for deciding when to do a more informational intervention (where the task is congruent with the client's meaning-making system) and when to go for a more transformational shift due to the client's challenges, requires a more complex way of making meaning.

If Kegan's model resonates, study it in depth. Keep in mind that it's just a model. Study it seriously and hold it lightly.

To gain an appreciation of the model, we need an appreciation of what is meant, in this context, by the terms *subject* and *object*.

SUBJECT

When you are subject to something that something *has you*. You can't see it, you don't have choice about it and you can't relate to it. You can be subject to an assumption about how the world works, a belief, cultural norms, a relational issue, etc. When you are subject to an assumption, it means that you are viewing the world *through* that assumption. In other words the assumption is invisible to you since you can't step back and look at it. You can also be subject to a trait or capacity. One example would be the client who was had by her hallucinations and who learned to have *them* instead through my use of the automatic imagination model.

Another example of a subject-object shift at the level of behavior is John Grinder's "breathing pattern", where the stutterer discovers that he has a distinctly different breathing pattern when he stutters as opposed to when he speaks fluently. This discovery helps turn the breathing patterns into *objects*, so that he can have choice about when to do what.

OBJECT

Object is the opposite of subject. Something is an object when we can look at it, investigate it, relate it to something and thereby have more choice about it.

That something is object doesn't mean that you have to hold it in conscious awareness. The client who learned to *have* her hallucinations (object) instead of being *had by* them (subject) doesn't have to consciously "watch it" all the time. Her choice-making is unconscious and she knows that she can step back and tweak it if need be.

Rumor has it that when the first movie was shown in 1886, the audience panicked when they saw a train coming towards them. They thought that the train was going to run over them. However, once you understand where the movie comes from, you know that no matter what happens the shark from the movie will never bite you, the train won't run you over and the gangster's bullet will never hit you.

This insight is an example of a subject-object shift, and

paradoxically helps you have the choice of letting go and getting absorbed into the suggested experience, feeling the excitement while simultaneously knowing that it's not real.

The person who has had this insight can also choose to study a movie in a detached way.

The same goes for thoughts and emotions. Someone with no perspective on their thoughts will be completely had by them and they will be confused with reality itself. Compare this to the person who has enough perspective on his thinking to realize that thoughts are just thoughts. He will have a hell of a lot more choice about "going there" or not—the same amount of choice as the moviegoer who realizes that it's just a movie.

When an entire meaning-making system moves from that which unquestionably runs me to something I can realize is "just a thought" then I have experienced a transformation of consciousness to a new system.

Kegan's model has four (we are skipping childhood here) forms of mind that adults may be operating out of. In each of these forms of mind we are subject to some things and can take other things as object. When what was subject becomes object of the new subject you have a new form of mind.

It may help a little to step back and consider the magical thinking of early childhood.

My niece, Anna, is four years old. In the past she would sometimes ask to speak with me when I spoke with my sister, Karine, on the phone. According to Karine, Anna would often gesture and point to things in the room as if I could see exactly what she saw. Jean Piaget discovered that this form of magical thinking is typical for young children. Typical examples of magical thinking would be to think that because I can't see myself when covering my eyes that means that others can't see me either. Or to think, when looking down on cars from a plane, that the cars actually are that small.

Children who operate this way are subject to their impulses and perceptions. When children learn to take their perceptions and impulses as objects, their thinking becomes much more concrete. They can now hold the idea of "durable objects", the notion that things in the world retain the same qualities over time. When the airplane takes off and the cars below look smaller, they aren't actually shrinking.

This shift in meaning-making is huge. A common assumption is that while kids make huge qualitative shifts in the way they know what they know, adults supposedly don't evolve. The work of people like Kegan, Loevinger, and Cook-Greuter show that some people evolve in adulthood and that the difference in perspective-taking between two thirty-year-olds can be as profound as the subject-object shift from magical thinking to holding durable categories. According to Kegan's model there are four discovered adult forms of mind in which the subject-object shift is as profound as the magical thinking-to-durable categories example. Those are the self-sovereign mind, the socialized mind, the self-authoring mind and the self-transforming mind. Most people operate in some mid-zone between systems. For adults, this is most typically between the socialized and self-authored minds.

FROM RAGE TO MULTIPLE ORGASMS

Samantha was a woman in her early twenties who was violent towards her boyfriend during her fits of rage. She was afraid that her boyfriend would break up with her if she didn't change, so she requested my help.

I started off by asking her *when* she did her raging, and she initially seemed confused and had a hard time noticing any pattern. Her answers were along the lines of "it just happens" and "he pisses me off, and then I get mad".

219

As we continued to explore *when* and *how* she did her raging, she only focused on what he did and didn't do that "got her mad". At no point did she talk about her inner life of thoughts, interpretation and emotions and neither did she talk about what she thought he was experiencing internally. She was hoping to change—that I could change her through hypnosis.

Quite early on I suspected that Samantha was mostly operating out of a self-sovereign mind.

Someone who operates out of a self-sovereign mind is *subject* to his own wants, needs and interests. What that means is that person will "know" others through the filter of his or her interests, wants and needs and cares about others only to the extent that their views and actions hinder or help their own interests.

They may of course be well aware what other people want and are interested in, but blind to how their "knowing" of others is done through the filter of their own wishes and interests.

If this is how I make meaning I have the capacity to recognize that you have a different perspective than mine, but I can't hold both perspectives simultaneously. Others become, in essence, "suppliers to the self", and I am unlikely to be motivated by abstract notions such as loyalty or commitment to a relationship. Hence the tendency for those with self-sovereign minds to objectify others and for their relationship to be exploitative in nature.

If I'm stuck in my own perspective, true compassion or self-reflection will be difficult since there is no sense of a psychological self over time. I *am* my interests, needs and wants.

Samantha, when talking about feelings, used terms like "pissed" and "mad" and seemed to have no awareness that she was an active participant in creating her own rage. It was something that *he* was responsible for by "pissing her off".

With some help from me, through my questioning, she saw that she essentially raged when he didn't do what she wanted.

Those who view others as suppliers of the self will likely have their anger issues when the other doesn't supply properly and doesn't do as the self-sovereign person wants.

I picked up two particularly interesting things. Samantha talked about love and how she wanted love and how she became violent when she didn't get love. When I asked her how she knew she was loved, she said she felt loved when she had power over her boyfriend and he did what she wanted.

Notice the passivity: love is something she gets when she is powerful and he does what she wants. What she calls love is linked to being in control and having power over another person.

At one point she started crying and said she felt bad about acting the way she did and that she felt bad for him. Out of curiosity I asked how she felt bad and if she felt guilty. She said that she did feel guilty. However, what she called "guilt" was once again all about her. She could see that he was hurt by her violence, and she felt bad because she feared he might leave her.

Structurally, it's the same type of "guilt" as that of the prisoner I recently spoke to. He talked about feeling bad and guilty about slapping another prisoner—not because he had hurt someone else or breached some internal standard, but because it could have interfered with his parole date.

Samantha's guilt and regret was also all about the potential negative consequences for her. She cared that her boyfriend felt bad to the extent that his feeling bad had direct consequences for her.

A couple of other things I detected/projected were that she seemed like a risk taker, a bit of an adrenalin junkie and adventurer. We had great rapport and she had high hypnotic capacity evidenced by her displays of absorption and suggestibility. When she described past events she "went there" as if she was reliving it with full congruence. When I described suggested experiences she easily got absorbed into those and she responded to my embedded commands in a non-volitional way.

My hunch was that change would happen during that session or not, that she likely wouldn't do homework, and likely would not have the patience for several sessions. I felt that our best shot at change was to utilize her high hypnotic capacity, use drama, use a highly emotional experience, and utilize her "need" for power and control. I did not attempt to move her towards a more socialized mind, but rather designed an intervention that fit her unique tendencies and self-sovereign mind.

I provoked her by calling her a sucker and pointed out that her boyfriend had all the power. That he had to behave a certain way for her to be in control so she could feel loved meant that he was the one in control, not her.

She reasoned with this and was intrigued when I suggested that a truly powerful person could trigger the feeling in herself without his help, and that if she started with the feeling of "love" it would be easier to get what she wanted from him...and it wouldn't matter that much anymore.

Here I am utilizing her perceived need for control and love and offering to teach her how to both be more self-sufficient and better at getting him to do what she wants.

(I suggest you go back and re-read the chapter where I evoked strong feelings of attraction.)

I used the exact same format here to evoke the feeling of being loved, had her imagine viewing her boyfriend and his behaviors through that filter, then gave her some suggestions that linked his "anger-inducing" facial expressions and voice tone to the feeling of being loved.

It worked beautifully. When later in the session I had her imagine those facial expressions and "defiant" voice tone, she automatically went into the state of "love". She was very enthusiastic about her new and improved control that didn't depend on him doing what she wanted.

She was so enthusiastic that she said that if only she could have orgasms the same way she wouldn't need him anymore.

Without missing a beat, I told her that she could produce her own orgasms the same way. I looked at her intensely and said, "When you begin to...*feel* those *sensations*...that let you know you're about to *have an orgasm*...when you *feel that now*...what's the first sensation you feel?" Samantha's breathing shifted, her face color changed and she pointed to her vagina and said she felt a cold sensation.

I asked "What's the next thing you feel as *it gets more intense now*...." At this point she was on the verge of coming. She stayed there for a while before I suggested that I would count from one to five and at the count of five I would touch her shoulder and she would have the deepest orgasm she was capable of.

She came hard and deep. It's hard to say who was the most blown away by this. She was ecstatic and said it was the best orgasm she had ever had, clearly this was way outside of what she thought possible.

I pretended that this was the most natural thing in the world. I had read about hypnotically evoked orgasms, but I had never done anything like this before. She was blissed and I was curious. I told her that she could have instant orgasms with no buildup and suggested that when I walked over and touched her shoulder, she would instantly come again. She did.

Finally, I "transferred" the "power" to her and suggested

223

that whenever she intended to have an orgasm and touched her own shoulder the same way, she would come. She proceeded to give herself multiple orgasms in my office with no further assistance from me whatsoever. She is probably the most blissful woman to ever leave my office.

I hadn't really planned to evoke the orgasms and while I had no reservations doing it, it did seem a bit outrageous when I looked back on it. I explained the whole thing to my wife when I got home and she was OK with it. I think she got from my vibe that there wasn't anything unethical or exploitative going on.

Samantha was supposed to show up for a scheduled follow-up a week later. She didn't show up. Neither did she answer the phone when I called her. There has been no feedback and I honestly don't know if she was a bit freaked out by the experience to the point where she didn't want to return. Or perhaps she had gotten what she came for (and then some) and didn't return, nor notify me, since she no longer saw me as relevant as a supplier to the self.

JAKE THE DRUNK DRIVER

Not long ago I had a conversation with a young man named Jake. Jake had spent a couple of months in jail for drunk driving and speeding. The first month in jail he had been deeply depressed, and a prison psychologist had helped him snap out of his depression in one day. I was curious to know the story, and I think that what the psychologist did was superb and demonstrated a wisdom and insight in working with a self-sovereign mind. There could be an element of luck as well.

Jake was twenty-two years old and had been part of the

Norwegian welfare system as a full-timer since he was seventeen. The welfare folks would find some job for him which he would take on and then promptly quit. He felt entitled to the money and didn't think he was "paid" enough. Furthermore he was very angry at the welfare folks for not finding the right job for him. He bragged about how he had exercised his power recently when his welfare check hadn't been in the mail on time. He had called the consultant on the case and threatened that if the money hadn't arrived in three days what Anders Behring Breivik (the Norwegian mass murderer) had done would be peanuts compared to what he would do.

Thankfully for him (or not) the consultant didn't report the threat. I provoked him a bit by pointing out how he was living as a parasite, and that it wasn't the welfare state's job to feed him and to find the right job for him, but that it was his job to do both rather than whine, sit on his ass and live off other people's hard-earned tax money. Judging from his response, it seemed no-one had ever talked straight and told him what most people probably think.

Jake regretted the drunk driving and speeding, but only the aspect of getting caught.

The psychologist must have recognized his short time horizon since her intervention didn't ask for more than he could handle. She gave him a simple explanation of what depression was and gave him a short chapter to read about depression from a book. She then tasked him with generating three short-term things to either accomplish or look forward to each week and to spend a couple of minutes every day anticipating happiness. I don't know the details, but as far as I can recall some goals had to do with work he was doing in jail, and others were looking forward to his parents and a couple of friends visiting him.

Depression often has much to do with expectations, and here he learned that he could set short-term goals and do

225

something to shift his own experience. And there were things he could do that didn't involve exploiting or manipulating others. I'm glad he wasn't sold a "chemical imbalance" story or a "blame your childhood" story, but rather one that emphasized his own expectations and actions in a way that fit his short time horizon.

THE SELF-SOVEREIGN CLIENT

To be blunt, I prefer not to work with these clients. As a group they are disproportionately represented when it comes to no-shows, last-minute cancellations and not paying. They are often very tough to work with as well. For this reason I do sometimes take them on to challenge myself. In my experience they relatively seldom seek my services and when they do it's usually for concrete issues like smoking cessation or stuttering. Of those who do seek help quite a few do so to provide themselves with an alibi to get a nagging spouse off their back. When I detect this, I decline working with them.

To work effectively with self-sovereign clients within their form of mind I have found the following ideas useful:

- Appeal to their short-term focus on self-centeredness and control.

The "sucker frame" I used with Samantha has often been useful, and I offer to teach them better ways to get what they want with less hassle from others. Often NLP-style state-based interventions using physiology, guided imagery and anchoring combined with rehearsing new behavioral responses work well.

- Get good at hypnosis.

These clients don't think in term of themes, nor do they self-reflect, so working with them to change their interpretations, stories and philosophy can often be an exercise in frustration. But at a more primary process level you can often do great work using hypnosis to anchor resourceful states to trouble contexts as well as rehearsing new behaviors. Changing sub-modalities and playing with association and dissociation can also be useful.

When working with teenagers who stutter I often combine Grinder's breathing pattern (described earlier) and hypnotic rehearsal of new states and behaviors as well as having them do behavioral tasks in public.

If you do timeline therapy, hypnotic age regression and/ or my version (described in detail in my book *Provocative Hypnosis*) then working at a primary process level works best. Keep it concrete; emphasize sub-modality shifts and behavioral responses.

• Emphasize the behavioral.

Whether it's exposure therapy to change a phobia, exercising to lift a depressed mode, or deliberately stuttering in public as a forum of symptom prescription, it's often easier to reach these clients at a behavioral level than using a more psychological approach. New code NLP offers some useful choices in utilizing games and movement to create flow states, which then can be linked to the contexts where they have struggled.

• Get good at provocation.

I honed my skills at provocation during my year working with the long-term unemployed. You may have to be willing to use "locker room language" to get credibility with these clients combined with some "tough love". The ability to set political correctness aside and confront them (with some humor and compassion in the mix) about their bullshit and manipulative tactics can help you connect where more formal and proper therapists have failed. I highly recommend both Milton Erickson and Frank Farrelly's work as excellent sources here.

There are a few things I would advise you not to do, or at least minimize:

- Don't get too psychological.

If you get too abstract and philosophical with these clients you risk losing them. Talking about their childhood in the attempt to have them gain insight is likely to get you nowhere. Exploring the "inner self" or cuddling a metaphorical "inner child" will get you nowhere *fast*.

- Don't sit around passively while they take charge.

- Don't contribute to their irresponsibility, exploitation and victim mentality.

To be able to do this type of work you've got to have good boundaries. You've got to be able to clearly differentiate between your experience and their experience. This will allow you to be psychologically independent while simultaneously being connected to them. That way you won't "feel their pain" and assume responsibility for their stuff, and you won't hold them responsible for your experience around them. You need to be able to communicate directly and enforce boundaries. I'll give a concrete example: A couple of years ago I worked with a "wannabe rock star" with a serious anger problem. He would rage and sometimes get violent when someone disrespected him.

He didn't answer the phone when I called to ask where he was ten minutes after our scheduled appointment. He called me back fifteen minutes later, said he hadn't heard the phone due to playing loud music in the car and said he had overslept but would be at my office shortly.

If you put up with bullshit like this you're toast. I had

him come back later. When I discovered upon meeting him that he hadn't put money in my account nor brought cash as promised, I promptly escorted him to an ATM and had him hand me the cash.

Psychiatrists are often pure poison for folks who operate like this. They let them get away with murder and attribute their behaviors as "evidence of mental illness", then "feel their pain" in an attempt to be empathetic and understanding.

Notice in the case of the wannabe rock star how I model a way of enforcing boundaries and get what I want without resorting to anger or violence. If a self-sovereign client acts in a disrespectful manner, you have a golden opportunity to be a model of excellence for them.

The ability to set boundaries and create a framework and roles for the purpose of creating a learning context for the client are capacities that require the ability to be psychologically independent and connected simultaneously—the capacity for operating out of a self-authoring mind.

Along with the capacities I just mentioned, you need the ability to be directive and be comfortable with power and authority. Sometimes, as Neanderthal and politically incorrect as it may sound, you had better have the ability to be the alpha male or female in the relationship.

The Self-Sovereign Change Artist

Thankfully, there are probably very few people who operate as agents of change out of this form of mind. The lack of perspective-taking, compassion and self-reflection are a big handicap.

On the other hand there may be the occasional genius who may be able to do some powerful stuff with hypnosis due to a combination of natural ability and talent, wicked calibration skills, confidence and a willingness to be directive. A fearless risk-taker may reach some people and inspire dramatic healings. Unfortunately, what they do is likely to be power-driven and exploitative. I suspect that the few agents of change who operate here are most likely to be found amongst power hypnotists (who have limited training) and some pick-up artists/coaches.

WARNING

While the self-sovereign person may seem simple-minded and shallow to those who have evolved past this point, do not confuse a self-sovereign mind with stupidity—the person could be a genius. Whether we are talking about street smarts, business brilliance or academic talent, this person may be highly intelligent. They can sometimes have a brilliant ability to detect and utilize opportunities, and since they are often impulsive and willing to take risks they are not burdened by the doubts and ambiguities that may hinder others. Combined with some luck and brainpower, these folks can often do quite well. They may also be good in physical emergencies and excel in jobs that are straightforward and where there is a direct short-term link between external rewards and external results.

The point is that no matter if they have a genius-level IQ, that intelligence will be constrained to be used in the service of achieving short-term pleasures and benefits by a person who is subject to his or her wishes, needs and interests.

TOWARDS A SOCIALIZED MIND

In his book *Redirect*, social psychologist Timothy Wilson writes about many surprising findings about how many social programs based on "common sense" not only don't work but have harmful consequences. However, when it comes to reducing teenage pregnancies and crime, volunteer community service has a documented effect.

The most plausible explanation for this has to do with the fact that most of those in these categories don't feel as if they are part of society. It's well-known that we often change our psychology as a result of observing our behavior when we behave differently.

By acting and behaving as if they care about other people, volunteers begin to actually care and identify with other people. They come to feel that they are part of society and society has become part of them. They have gone from being pre-socialized to being socialized.

I have to admit that I don't think I have played much of a part in helping people make this change in my private practice.

However, as a martial arts/self-defense instructor, I am convinced that I have played a part in many young people making a transition from a self-sovereign to a socialized mind without intending to do so.

If I were to speculate, I think it's plausible, as in Timothy Wilson's example, that those helped to make this transition

231

were likely already operating in a mid-zone between the two forms of mind.

The transformation into a socialized mind seems to have two essential elements:

1. A bringing inside the self of other people's perspectives which formerly were only considered from one's own interests and wishes.

2. The ability to make those internalized perspectives an essential ingredient in how one's sense of self is constructed, instead of only being concerned with what someone holding those views will do as a consequence of one's actions.

Instead of being subject to the individual's interests, these needs and interests become the object of a larger self—a self that *has* needs and interests instead of being had by them.

For the self-sovereign mind, conflict is external and other people's views are held "outside" and are troublesome to the extent they get in the way of "what I want".

When I internalize others' perspectives, my sense of self gets constructed in the relationship between my views and another's. How significant others view me becomes an essential ingredient in how I view myself.

Now I become subject to the internalized values, beliefs and roles derived from outside sources. A religious orientation, political ideology and its internalized principles and assumptions become a filter through which I view the world. It doesn't have to be religious or political ideology. I may become an environmentalist or view the world through the internalized framework of some profession.

At this point I develop the capacity to hold several perspectives simultaneously, be self-reflective about my actions and the actions of others, and become loyal and devoted to something larger than myself. With this comes the ability to experience guilt and internal conflict.

Developmental psychologist Jennifer Garvey Berger, in her excellent book *Changing on the Job*, makes a very intriguing point.

Most coaching and psychotherapy interventions presuppose a socialized or self-authored mind. Coaches, often passionate, strive to help people discover their own inner voice and authority. While a key task in coaching the socialized mind, Garvey Berger claims that it's the wrong approach for coaching someone with a self-sovereign mind and can even be anti-developmental.

Garvey Berger points out that those operating out of a self-sovereign mind have not yet internalized the voices of important others and therefore cannot disentangle themselves because they have not been entangled in the first place. Encouraging the clients to focus on their own opinions may result in them ignoring their connection to significant others; the task is to find that their own inner voice can blend and merge with those around them.

In many ways Garvey Berger's message is deeply unsettling to me and intuitively feels wrong. As far back as I can remember, I have valued personal freedom and my political and ideological preferences have been strongly libertarian. As an agent of change I have viewed my role as one where my job is to create learning contexts where people discover that their symptoms aren't happening *to* them, but are something they largely create through how they think, interpret and make sense of experience. You could say that I have largely been committed to helping people become more self-authoring.

In light of this it's no wonder that Garvey Berger's proposal feels flat-out wrong. But that doesn't mean that she *is* wrong. Listening to be unsettled—to allow deeply held convictions to be challenged—and exploring taken-for-granted assumptions in as honest and feedback-rich a way as possible are important keys in taking as object old and deep assumptions that have had me.

Is it really true that those who operate out of a self-sovereign mind need to evolve into a socialized mind before they can become self-authoring?

Could someone go from a self-sovereign into a self-authored form of mind without having to pass through a socialized mind?

I honestly don't know.

One interesting point to consider is how independent researchers such as Jane Loevinger, Clare Graves and Robert Kegan have reached remarkably similar conclusions. They all discovered a form of mind similar to the self-sovereign mind described here. They all discovered a socialization process where the person internalizes the perspectives of his or her cultural surround on the way towards a self-authored mind that has remarkably similar conceptualization across the disciplines.

Throughout the last few years I have given much thought to how I have seemingly been a lot more successful in helping my martial arts students make this transition compared to my private practice clients.

Quite a few parents have either called me or stopped me on the street to tell me how their teenager or young adult has become a lot more socialized as a result of training with me.

These parents have often talked about their teenager "growing up", improving their grades in school and maturing. Some have talked about their son no longer getting into fights or trouble with the law.

I've often been puzzled by the fact that I have seemed to "produce" well-adjusted conformists even when my teaching and philosophy has been very much about thinking for oneself and challenging authority and tradition.

From a developmental perspective the following seems to be a plausible explanation for how the gradual shift occurs.

In a sports club or martial arts school, the student who might have gotten into fights on the streets still gets to fight and be competitive. He gets met where he's at. However, to get what he wants he has to take his training partners' interests into account. For those who compete, there are rules, a referee and disciplined preparations to be made. They learn to manage their anger and fear. There is also a philosophy to internalize.

Over time the internalized philosophy becomes an essential ingredient in how their sense of self is constructed. The student will likely identify with his instructors and team so they also become part of who he is.

Applied to change work, when transitioning towards a socialized mind it's important that the coach recognizes that there are both losses (seldom acknowledged) and gains in transformational change. As Kegan often has pointed out "The bridge needs to be anchored at either side."

The losses are likely to be about fear of losing freedom and independence as well as confusion in discovering a more complex world.

And you had better recognize that it's not a coincidence that teenagers internalize some ideology and so many prisoners find organized religion.

Part of the person's likely evolution seems to be to internalize outside perspectives, identify with one or several groups, then co-construct his sense of self out of that.

In my mind this means that you should be willing to offer a philosophy that these people can internalize. I realize that I am "swearing in church" in the eyes of much of the NLP world, where working with the structure of experience while *not* dealing with content is so deeply valued.

I do often teach principles and philosophies based on

235

Albert Ellis's REBT and William Glasser's Choice Theory as well as basic NLP presuppositions. The client can internalize a philosophy or combination of philosophies that emphasize reason, autonomy and the value of relationships.

For the few clients I see in this mid-zone I will often use the prescribing musturbation pattern after pushing them to the edge of their meaning-making. Often we end up with something like "I need respect" and my job (usually difficult) is to begin to help them to relativize what was absolute, to help them gain perspective on their perceived needs and to open up for other perspectives. A meditation practice where the person learns to observe thoughts and feelings and name their emotions can help here.

When doing hypnotic regression work I will "anchor a bridge on either side" by both speaking to their "what's in it for me right now" side and invite them to notice/ask questions about how others may view the situation and the effect on them. Helping them step into others' perspectives during a hypnotic process can be powerful.

•   •   •

Celine was a woman in her mid-twenties who came in for anger issues around the time I worked with Samantha. She also did some heavy raging and occasionally resorted to violence towards her boyfriend.

Like Samantha, she also said that she felt bad and guilty. I couldn't help but notice that where Samantha exclusively talked about her own needs and viewed her boyfriend as a supplier to the self, Celine talked about feeling bad about her boyfriend's sadness and held herself responsible for his sadness and anxiety. Her guilt stemmed from breaching internalized values around hurting others.

She also held her boyfriend responsible for "making her angry".

This simultaneous "over-responsibility" (holding herself directly responsible for his emotional state) and "under-responsibility" (holding him responsible for how she feels) is a natural consequence when someone operates out of a socialized mind. When my sense of self is constructed from the relationship between how I view myself and how I think you view me, then you can say that I am *made up* by my relationships. With this self-construction it's extremely difficult to not take significant others' rejection and criticism personally. If I am in a relationship and my self is co-constructed in such a way, then my significant other's criticism or rejection is deeply personal; it's a rejection of *me*.

The only way I can take it less personally would be to get colder and distance myself from the other person. Clichés about my "better half" come from this form of mind. If I need my partner to complete me by being "my better half" then the idea of "one soul" may be appealing, and difference in and of itself may be threatening.

Celine was angry at her boyfriend for his lack of initiative and presence. He would "shut down" when she got angry and she would rage even more.

She had internalized the notion of a traditional feminine role as the one she wanted, and therefore she needed her boyfriend to adopt more of a traditional masculine role to complete her. She didn't quite put it that way, but she completely resonated and lit up when I mentioned it.

I teased her a bit about being the man in the relationship and challenged her to be a strong woman. Instead of waiting for her boyfriend to change, I suggested that she turn on his masculinity by becoming more of the woman in the relationship.

I tasked her with doing three distinct "feminine" things in relation to her boyfriend every day for a certain time period. She was also instructed to brainstorm options and behaviors with her girlfriends to turn the whole thing into a light-hearted and playful game.

She started doing things like calling him at work and asking how he was doing. She dressed more seductively at times and held a baby on a flight they were on.

Where a person operating from a self-sovereign mind will manipulate and exploit to meet her short-term interests, the socialized mind is likely to attempt to adjust her own behavior so that it is in alignment with gender and social roles she has internalized.

Celine did not have much hypnotic capacity and wasn't good at using her imagination to access states. Therefore a behavioral intervention was the best choice available. Here the intervention was adapted to fit within her socialized mind and didn't attempt to get her to become more self-authored.

Behaving in accordance with some internalized role is achievable with a socialized mind. To those who operate here the idea of personal responsibility is likely to be conceptualized as behaving according to those roles and expectations, whether that's being punctual or keeping one's promises.

For the self-authoring mind, notions of personal responsibility are not about "doing the right thing". Rather it's about deciding for oneself what the "right" thing is and behaving in accordance with that. In Celine's case, a transformational intervention would entail stepping back and reflecting upon gender roles and authoring for herself what it means to be a woman in a relationship.

Here I do have long-term feedback in the form of a letter from a very happy couple a year and a half later. Their relationship was much happier, and her raging and violence were completely gone. And he had in fact become much more "masculine" in the relationship.

• • •

I remember bursting out in laughter when first studying the socialized mind. A number of screw-ups came to mind—screw-ups that were the result of presupposing self-authoring capacities in virtually all my clients due to not having a developmental perspective at the time.

The first example that came to mind was a few sessions with a Muslim woman that went nowhere. She had a deep internal conflict. Her parents wanted to arrange her marriage. She was dating a young Norwegian man and didn't dare tell her parents about it as they would not approve. She felt as if the conflict was tearing her in half. With a co-constructed sense of self made up by her relationships, no wonder she felt an "internal tearing", as if she was being pulled in two directions.

Guess what I did?

I attempted a visual squash or parts integration. This is an NLP format where I had her symbolically put the part of her that wanted to be with her Norwegian boyfriend and decide for herself on the palm of one hand, and the part that wanted to please her parents on the other. This intervention presupposed exactly the type of self she didn't have. I took for granted that she had a self that wasn't made up by her relationships. Rather I presupposed a self that could have a relationship *to* her relationships—a psychologically independent or autonomous self that had the parts and could mediate a conflict between them using her own self system or way of knowing.

Can you see the problem?

Ironically, if she'd had the type of self presupposed here,

239

she wouldn't experience an internal tearing due to her parents' and her own expectations being in conflict. But she *was* her relationships and didn't yet have a self that could *have* a relationship. This is why conflict is often so difficult for the socialized mind. A client whose parents and boyfriend have conflicting expectations may find herself completely bewildered and helpless to make a decision.

An approach that gradually had her step back and reflect on various values, principles and expectations she had been subject to might have helped to develop the ability to have relationships. But to expect a parts integration to work here is unrealistic. I'm not saying that a parts integration couldn't have been useful in helping her resolve a conflict that had to do with some habit. It's not so much the technique but the mismatch between her form of mind and the capacity for self-authorship she would need for such a technique to be helpful with that type of conflict.

MR. WALL STREET

Contrast Celine (with the raging issue) with an investor and trader in his early forties who had the capacity for self-authorship. His presenting issue was impotence. He was involved in multiple sexual relationships simultaneously, and the impotence was a factor with one of the women he was seeing. He had decent hypnotic capacity, and I guided him into a hypnotic experience. He had said he was conflicted; my role with him was to help "call forth" the various "parts" of him that were in conflict and to ask open questions to help the negotiation process. He generated his own solution. While his solution seemed bizarre to me, it worked for him and he was able to continue a sexual relationship with the same woman without any impotency issues. His conflict was about him not acting in accord with his own moral code.

•   •   •

A woman I know well attended a short NLP training and enjoyed the experience. At the time she was operating out of a socialized mind. She decided to book an appointment with the NLP instructor, who is a skilled and experienced instructor. He prefers mutuality in coaching relationships, doesn't like to impose content, and delights in working at the process level where the client can develop their own solutions.

This sounds wonderful to me and many others. It was a mismatch for this particular client. When the NLP instructor asked how she thought they should approach the issue, he quickly lost credibility in her eyes. She reasoned that he was the expert and that it was his job to select formats and teach her how to use her mind better. The democratic approach of making her an equal partner was interpreted to mean, perhaps unfairly, that he didn't know what he was doing.

My experience tells me that you have to be comfortable being an authority figure to reach many with a socialized mind. It's often useful with these clients to take charge and be comfortable with being the authority and expert that directs the other's experience.

To help someone begin to transition towards a more self-authoring mind, sometimes what's required is the paradoxical role of being the authority figure that instructs the client that it's time they start thinking for themselves. This is understandably not that appealing for agents of change who take for granted the self-authoring capacities of the client and who are especially sensitive about not imposing their own stuff or giving advice.

But from a developmental angle, many may see that adopting this role initially is a way of speaking to both "who the client is" and "who they are becoming" simultaneously.

DINNER WITH A MURDERER

I just had dinner with a murderer.

Adam knifed and killed a guy about ten years ago. He served three and a half years in jail and has since had additional convictions for severe violence. During our conversation I asked a number of questions, several of them with the intent of discovering the edges of his meaning-making.

Adam says he wants to change his life and credits the birth of his daughter as a key factor. Still, the birth of his daughter hasn't ended his criminal career, as he recently added a burglary conviction to his résumé.

The Norwegian correctional services have tried to help Adam change his ways through anger-management courses and group therapy. I'm sure those teaching the courses are well intended, even though Adam claims the courses haven't helped him at all. They have taught him versions of "counting from 1–10" in addition to talking about his feelings and exploring his past with other prisoners.

Here's the "funny" part. Adam claims his acts of violence weren't done in anger. Violence was just a cynical and effective tool for collecting money. During our conversation, despite me encouraging it, Adam never reached beyond the concrete world of his own needs and interests. No abstractions or talk about values, beliefs or themes.

When I probed for any guilt, empathy or compassion for the guy he killed, he talked about the consequences of being locked up in jail and referred to his actions as "a tragic situation". Adam seems stuck in a self-sovereign form of mind, and his capacities for perspective taking, self-reflection and empathy seem minimal.

Clearly, most adults who operate here don't kill people or live a life where violence is used to collect money. But probably most of those who live this way operate out of a self-sovereign mind. While it's clearly possible for self-sovereign folks *not* to be violent and live lives of crime, I wonder if it's possible to go from where he is to a law-abiding life without making a qualitative shift in meaning-making.

While I have minimal faith in typical anger-management courses like the ones Adam attended, I have even less faith that someone who hasn't reached at least a socialized mind will be able to benefit from them. Talking about one's childhood in a group and learning to count from one to ten won't do much to change the ways of someone who can use violence to serve his immediate needs without feeling anger or guilt. It's the wrong approach and one that seems to take for granted a way of understanding that Adam doesn't have.

As a big fan of mixed martial arts, and as a new father, he wants to fight competitively and get back to school. In my mind, this seems to be the way most likely to succeed, to help Adam reach a socialized mind where internalizing values and identifying with people may change his ways. I'm not sure much optimism is warranted.

Critics may protest and say that mixed martial arts training will make him a more dangerous and skilled fighter, and they will be correct. Others will conclude that he is a stone-cold psychopath and point out that there is little, if any, evidence that psychotherapy or anything else will help. They might say that he was likely born a psychopath and will die a psychopath. They may be correct.

However, a developmental angle offers a more optimistic interpretation in pointing out that what we call psychopathy seems, more often than not, to be an extreme case of adult meaning-making at a self-sovereign level without even the slightest move towards a socialized mind. There are likely other factors at play as well.

Can someone like Adam grow, with the right amount of challenge and support, to a new form of mind? I don't know, but if he can, the path of mixed martial arts, identification with teammates and the internalization of a good value system sounds like the best pace and lead I can think of.

Based on my conversations with the members of the prison population, it seems as if the majority of the repeat offenders are struggling somewhere in the transition between a self-sovereign and socialized mind.

According to Kegan, there are several studies that show that more adults are somewhere in the mid-zone between socialized and self-authoring minds. This completely resonates with my experience as an agent of change in private practice as well as my experience as both a participant and instructor at various seminars throughout the years. Before taking a development approach I would have categorized the two groups as different breeds of people. In recent years I have come to see that it's more useful and accurate to think of it as different systems of meaning-making.

I agree with Kegan when he says that much of coaching and psychotherapy presupposes the capacity for self-authorship. Kegan offers the following criteria for self-authorship:

- Perceive our standards as based on our own experience rather than upon the attitudes or desires of others.

- Perceive ourselves as evaluators of experience rather than regarding ourselves as existing in a world where the values are inherent in and attached to the object of our perceptions.

- Place the standards within ourselves, recognizing that the goodness or badness of any experience or perpetual object is not something inherent in that object, but a value we place on it.

- Transform our energies from manipulating the environment into developing greater and greater self-support.

- Learn to stand on our own feet emotionally, intellectually and economically.

- Learn to stop indoctrinating ourselves with the philosophies and values we imbibed in youth.

- Learn to challenge and question our own basic values and our own thinking, so that we really think for ourselves.

- Take responsibility for our lives.

- Learn the psychological myths or scripts that govern our behavior and re-author them for better insight of why the script is as it is.

Quite a list, huh?

Kegan offers this list in his book *Over Our Heads*, in a chapter on the undiscussed mental demands of psychotherapy.

In this chapter he writes extensively about a famous film where three legends in the psychotherapy world spend a session working with a woman named Gloria. The three therapists are Albert Ellis, Fritz Perls and Carl Rogers.

He makes several compelling points. One is that the three therapists operate out of different frameworks and have markedly different styles. He simultaneously points out that they all presuppose that Gloria has the capacity for self-authorship in the session, and that Gloria seems to operate out of a socialized form of mind. None of the famous therapists are able to help her much and Kegan more than implies a correlation between the lack of results and the therapy being over her head.

I disagree with Kegan in how he characterizes Ellis's work. He claims that Ellis is essentially just teaching people to talk to themselves differently. He writes that Ellis is unwittingly trying to get his client's mind into the same fourth order (self-authoring) shape. He further writes, "Since the behaviorist tradition rejects the notion of a self holistically or coherently directing our behavior, it is understandable that Ellis would confuse the mental behavior of the fourth order capacity with the structure of mind that gives rise to the behavior. Seeking the latter, he ends up teaching the former. Unfortunately, it's hard to talk people into a new order of consciousness."

I think this is an unfair and inaccurate assessment of Ellis and his REBT system. In fact, Ellis worked hard at getting clients to become aware of the musts, shoulds and oughts through which they were viewing the world and to make them visible so that they could be challenged and disputed. For me, Ellis's system has been very useful in helping people make transformative changes. I would like to invite you to go back and re-read the chapters about Maureen the Musturbator and the Religious Atheist.

In the first case I help Maureen take internalized *musts* and turn them into objects—the beginning of a transition between a socialized and a self-authoring mind.

In the case of the Religious Atheist, who was self-authoring, my purpose was to make visible some of the *musts* driving his self system.

In my mind these cases are great examples of combining REBT, NLP and hypnosis with an awareness of subject-object psychology.

At a seminar Kegan and Lisa Lahey held in Boston a few years ago, I asked Kegan what he would do differently if he could have a shot at Gloria. He said he would put more emphasis on the losses and fears she was dealing with in making the transition. He has a method called Immunity to Change that is designed to do that. I won't go into that process here, but rather refer you to his book of the same title.

I will say that the method is often an excellent choice when the client is facing challenges that require that the client evolve his or her meaning-making to master the challenge.

A typical example would be a person operating out of a socialized mind who gets promoted into a position where they have to deal with conflict and be self-initiating and self-correcting. Often these folks are paralyzed with fear.

In my experience, hypnotic regression work can often be more effective in helping people make these types of transformative changes by identifying some prototype context, then having the unconscious bring up the emotion that stops them from X. Using the emotion as an affect bridge so that old reconstructed memories, assumptions and emotions can be updated often removes the "blocks" that prevent them from naturally evolving to deal with the challenges at hand and activating a bigger meaning-making system.

While developmental theory says that these shifts from one system to another happen gradually over time and are developed, I have had experiences using hypnotic regression work (the format in *Provocative Hypnosis*) that suggests that more evolved systems can be activated as soon as old networks of unresolved emotion and fixed ideas are resolved.

As far as I know I'm the only one out there who has combined developmental psychology and hypnotic regression work with the intent of helping people make transformations to a bigger meaning-making system. Part of my motivation of writing this book is to inspire more people to explore along the same lines.

Unfortunately, Kegan, Cook-Greuter, Cowan and some

others don't seem to have looked into hypnosis and hypnotic regression work. They are missing out and don't know it.

Let me be specific. Re-read the last mental demand of self-authorship on Kegan's list—the one about learning the psychological myths or scripts that govern our behavior and re-authoring them.

Kegan is spot on when he observes that when the socialized mind is involved in exploring the link between past events and current symptoms and unhelpful patterns they can often have powerful *Aha!* experiences and insights. But what they can't do is to then re-author their own experience. They may instead learn more and more about "why" they are such a mess and become a better informed audience member rather than a more competent script writer and director.

Hypno-analysis and hypnotic regression work is often amazingly effective in cleaning phobias, specific fears, anger issues and psychosomatic issues like migraines, allergies and a host of other issues. Not only is it usually way more effective than the psychoanalysis and regular "talk therapy", it's also a hell of a lot faster. And those with socialized minds also change.

I urge anyone to get their hands on tapes of Dave Elman doing hypno-analysis in the fifties and sixties. When he introduced his techniques to physicians when teaching them hypnosis, his results were often mind-blowing.

If you listen to Ellman's work with an NLP background and some insight into the reconstructive nature of memory, then you may be really turned off by the content impositions. And from a developmental perspective, it's clear that Elman provides the self-authoring voice his clients lack, and that they internalize his interpretations, which then become "as real as real" at an emotional level due to the hypnosis.

Self-authoring and self-transforming minds can also more easily re-author their stories in hypnosis. It would be interesting to see if Elman had been able to adapt had he had more clients with these ways of understanding.

A JOHN GRINDER FLAW?

I have gotten tremendous value both personally and professionally from John Grinder's teachings. As a long-time student and fellow explorer I think it's only fair that I challenge his ideas and encourage other students to do the same.

When I first met John back in 2003 I was deeply impressed by his brilliance and wisdom, and I still am to this day. When he came to Norway in 2005 we really connected and he mentored me for five or six years.

One of the first things he said that first day in Oslo was that all beliefs are limiting.

I immediately asked him if he believed that, and he cracked a smile and invited me to play. I think one factor in us resonating so well together was that he didn't get defensive, but playfully engaged with all my challenges—very unusual for me—and he appreciated someone questioning his ideas and being willing to test anything through direct experience.

John deconstructs and rips apart pretty much everything. If students ask about beliefs, John will point out that all beliefs are limiting. Identity, according to John, is a deep trap. Dare bring up topics such as values, self-concept, truth, or even right or wrong and John will scoff at the concepts and rip them apart.

Don't get him started on ideology.

He deconstructs these notions and points out that they are arbitrary linguistic constructs that we impose on the flow of experience and which take us further away from direct experience.

For me it was perfect timing. I'm a guy with strong self-authoring capacities, so who could be better than a wizard like John at helping me shake up my personal authority, identity and cherished beliefs?

Where I was busy helping my clients realize how made up and arbitrary were the ideas they had internalized from their family, religion and outside sources, John was helping me realize how my sense of core self and personal authority was as arbitrary and made up as anything else.

But what about the vast majority of seminar participants who operate out of a socialized mind and those in the midzone between socialized and self-authoring minds? Many are just beginning to construct for themselves all the stuff that John is busy deconstructing.

For someone taking the courageous first steps of questioning taken-for-granted assumptions and beliefs who's just starting to distinguish what they believe from what they where *taught* to believe, is it useful to be told that all beliefs are limiting...full stop.

Is it useful to tell those who are beginning to construct their own identity apart from their peer group that identity is a deep trap?

While I think this deconstruction can be very useful for those who have self-authoring capacities, I suspect that it's more often than not anti-developmental for many others. I think that critical thinking skills, using reason to learn to adjust expectations, questioning and testing beliefs, etc., may be more valuable.

John's solution, in his New Code approach, is the new code change format, which consists of selecting some context where we most strongly experience X—to step into the imagined context on a piece of paper (to spatially anchor) and feel the feelings.

After breaking state, the clients are then instructed to

play a game (alphabet, NASA, etc.) designed to produce a high-performance state. When the agent of change calibrates that the client is in a high-performance state, the client is instructed to step back into the context without consciously attempting to influence the experience.

This is as close to a content-free intervention as you can get. The client will unconsciously generate his own solutions (which often surprise him) by activating a high-performance state whenever they step into a similar context.

This way of working can be extremely useful, and entering a "know-nothing" state can generate solutions that are more useful than those generated from an "I know" state.

Changing one's state can open up new worlds, and after attending seminars with Kegan, Cook-Greuter (ego development), Cowan and Todorovic (Spiral Dynamics). I have been somewhat puzzled that exploring the power of shifts in state in relation to meaning-making doesn't seem to be part of the curriculum.

On the other hand, after spending long periods new-coding anything with a pulse, my experience is that a new code intervention—as a stand-alone process—will likely not help someone make a qualitative shift in meaning-making.

As an explorer, don't take my word for this—test it for yourself.

Would the new code change format help Adam the murderer to become a better money collector? What would his high-performance state be used in service of? Would he find other ways of satisfying his short-term interests? Might he get better at compassion and perspective-taking?

There is only one way to find out.

In *Whispering In the Wind*, co-authored by Carmen Bostic St.Clair, Grinder offers the following: "The question is not what is real; the question is in how many ways can we appreciate that which surrounds us."

251

Someone outside of ideology who is keenly aware of not just how limiting it is to have an inner system of beliefs and values, and who is untroubled by paradox, can see multiple layers on every issue and hold different perspectives simultaneously. For this person there is no one truth to be locked into, but some approaches may be more useful to act as if they were true in a particular context.

Someone like John will playfully want to experience and learn as much as possible.

Having seen many "new code oriented practitioners" that likely operate mostly out of a socialized mind, the postmodern rhetoric gets turned into a sort of hyper-relativism where nothing is true or better than anything else. The result is often a belief that there is little to learn and no reason to question beliefs since "there is no truth" to be found. Often people end up relativizing other perspectives to defend their own absolutism. Some end up unable to make decisions and in "action paralysis" due to being afraid to impose content. Hyper-relativism can become a straight jacket.

BE AWARE

Some final points regarding the socialized mind:

• Don't confuse it with establishment beliefs.

People, depending on many factors, can internalize all sorts of ideologies. Some may internalize anti-establishment conspiracy theories and view the world through those. Some may internalize a philosophy that values personal responsibility and freedom, such as Ayn Rand's objectivism, and therefore seem very independent. But a lot of what looks like autonomy isn't. If the person has internalized, say, Rand's philosophy of rugged individualism and attempts to be an individualist on Rand's terms, then we are still talking about a socialized mind.

- Don't be confused by postmodern rhetoric.

A few years ago I saw a TV documentary about the nature vs. nurture debate. One participant was a Norwegian professor who claimed that outside of the sexual organs, all gender differences were socially constructed. His students spouted postmodern rhetoric about diversity, multi-culturalism and truth being socially constructed, and they did it with the intensity of religious fundamentalists. They wouldn't even consider more biological explanations and reacted with anger and stonewalling when their cherished beliefs were challenged. The "other side" consisting of, amongst others, Charles Murray of *The Bell Curve* fame, did not spout postmodern rhetoric. He talked more about reason, facts and objectivity, but also acknowledged social, cultural and system factors without a trace of defensiveness. Murray demonstrated much more of a both/and perspective and was willing to challenge his assumptions.

- Don't confuse it with kindness or (necessarily) valuing other people.

It's true that the socialized mind's ability to become part of society by having society become part of him makes a civilized society possible.

It's also the home of "the good German", who having internalized Nazism, "just followed" orders in executing Jews. It's the home of uncritical nationalism and patriotism that can easily result in duty, honor, country and "my country right or wrong".

If Adam the murderer were to internalize Islam or some white supremacy ideology, neither he nor the rest of us would be any safer from his violence.

253

- Make a distinction between style and structure.

A very hands-on "tough as nails" army sergeant, leader or psychologist can operate out of a socialized mind. They don't need to be "nice" and sensitive or politically correct. Their authority is derived from their role, their superiors or the company/organization's code or tradition.

I recently saw a mid-level manager who was tough and directive with those under him in the hierarchy. As soon as he had to deal with his superiors, he turned into an obedient ass-kisser.

THE SOCIALIZED AGENT OF CHANGE

The socialized agent of change will derive authority from his role and credentials. He will have internalized some school of thought or other and view his clients through that filter. He may view critical questions against that school of thought as personal attacks and feel a strong dichotomy between himself as expert and the client as the learner.

Hopefully the socialized coach has learned NLP so that he can work more on a process level. This way he may be able to help people who are more evolved.

In my opinion, someone who operates out of a socialized mind isn't really equipped for this line of work. He is likely to be over-responsible, resulting in holding himself responsible for his client's suffering. If he is present with his client and the client's suffering and then feels guilty for "causing it" he doesn't have healthy boundaries. Likewise, responding with defensive anger towards the client's behaviors and then blaming the client for "making him angry" is another boundary issue.

THE SELF-AUTHORING CLIENT
(AND COACH)

I have had some interesting conversations lately with a prisoner who is self-authoring.

Jim makes a compelling argument for having been convicted of a crime he didn't commit. A very successful businessman, he is fighting hard for the opportunity to clear his name, as well as for the survival of both his company and his employees. Not an easy life!

He had been promised he could spend the last six weeks of his prison time at home with an electronic device around his ankle. Murphy's Law seemed to be at work, and due to a bureaucratic screw-up and the games played between departments to save face and avoid taking responsibility, the opportunity slipped away. His wife is struggling with a sense of deep injustice and hopelessness. Add to this that he has been unsuccessful in his attempts to gain access to the Internet, access to more visits and phone time, and you get some tough realities and living conditions to handle.

He does get discouraged and depressed from time to time, but he has a tremendous strength. Actually, he has several— he is knowledgeable, well educated and intelligent. He also has a meaning-making system that constantly allows him to know (and experience) that his expectations and interpretations to a large extent determine how he feels. Not only that, he experiences himself (much of the time) as able to adjust and re-author those expectations and interpretations.

255

While the guards and administration pretty much treat him like shit, he isn't made up by their projections and expectations of who he is. While he "loses it" on occasion, he is mostly able to define his own role and stay constructive pursuing his self-defined goals.

When working with self-authored clients you can't hide behind diplomas or certificates; you've got to have the internal security to resonate with them. They may seek mutuality in the relationship and look for a guide or coach who can challenge them and support them in developing their own solutions.

Often I help them make visible the musturbatory demands inherent in their self system. At other times we do hypnotic regression work and update old memories that contribute to unwanted behavior, outdated responses and symptoms in present time.

Helping them explore dichotomies (either/or) in their map is often of tremendous value. The Nazi path angle, presented earlier, often reasonates.

Shadow work (presented in the next chapter) where they own and discover the "not me" aspects they project onto others, helps some of them develop some self-transforming capacities.

Let's get back to the self-authoring prisoner.

There are some typical limitations associated with this form of mind. Jim is used to negotiating deals with other leaders and entrepreneurial types in his industry. He has persuasion skills, competence, money and high social status. He values progress, pragmatism, results and ethics.

His self-authoring mind has a filter and is open to feedback, but because of his self system, the feedback had better fit within his frame.

Those with this form of mind are often ideological and convinced that others should see the world the way they do,

256

and that other adults are fundamentally self-authoring like them. They often think that any reasonable person can use reason to deal with the world in a close-to-objective way. But they can be blind to the subjectivity behind the objectivity.

Jim projects his world-view and meaning-making system upon the prison administration and guards, and he misses badly!

The socialized bureaucratic mind doesn't care about his arguments and reasoning. They view him as a prisoner and treat him according to protocol. Real-life consequences, or intentions and consequences not matching doesn't matter for those who view "doing their job" as following orders and who can't write their own definitions.

For them to do anything differently they would need instructions "from above". They think he's the unreasonable one. Besides, they believe in the legal system and anyone who attacks that system attacks who they *are*. If he weren't guilty, he wouldn't be here. Had he realized that these folks do not make meaning like he does, he might have changed his approach. Realizing he has no power at all, and that to the socialized mind it's his place in hierarchy that matters, he might have focused on making sure that he communicated his message to proper experts with proper authority in the prison system.

The self-authored mind's main limitation might very well be being fused with its filter and therefore projecting that filter onto persons who don't have those self-authoring capacities—that and the tendency to use feedback to sharpen one's own argument and stance. If a person spends his time with colleagues who share his premises, framework and ideology, then he will likely continue to be had by that framework and ideology.

JØRGEN RASMUSSEN

THE SELF-TRANSFORMING MIND

The author Fred Kofman often asks his seminar participants the question, "Have you ever met an idiot who thinks just like you?"

I love that question, and I am amused by the puzzled responses it evokes. Those who answer "no" may not have considered that they are claiming a 100% correlation between disagreeing with them and stupidity.

Jim—our self-authoring prisoner—values intelligence, and in his self system, intelligence and stupidity are clear-cut opposites. So are reason and unreason.

So what would happen if Jim had more of a self-transforming mind—one where the self as system was no longer subject but object, so that the self as system was transformative.

Instead of being a "thing", a complete, whole and stable self dealing with other whole and distinct selves in the world, we might talk more about *minding* and the process of *selfing*. The self becomes a fluid process of selfing where the boundaries of what constitutes self and other is recreated moment by moment instead of identifying exclusively with being an intelligent and reasonable person who is battling the stupid and irrational people out there.

Jim, on better days at least, may have come to reject the notion of the conflict, battle and stupidity being exclusively *out there*. This could have opened up the possibility for him

258

to see the stupidity in the intelligence and the intelligence in the stupidity.

The self-transforming mind has fewer dichotomies and thinks less in terms of polarities. It realizes that clarity and confusion, intelligence and stupidity, knowing and not knowing aren't distinct either/or but rather two sides of the same coin. This insight enables some people to then be cautious and wary of their own selfing and "I am" identifications, since any self-conceptualization must be incomplete *and* partial, and that the sense of a whole and complete core self is an illusion, a blunder that comes from confusing internal coherence with completeness.

The insight about how any self-identification projects the "not me" out there to play the role of the other end of a polarity opens the opportunity for conflict between self and other to be the spark for recovering more of one's complexity.

Having dinner with Adam the murderer offers me the opportunity to be unsettled. How can spending time with him potentially be a transformative experience? To what extent can I acknowledge that writing about him and defining him as a murderer influences who I further project him to be and which motives and traits I attribute to him? And how does him being the murderer and the violent, exploitative and manipulative menace to society enable me to attach the opposite qualities onto my sense of self? To what extent can I acknowledge that there is much more to both of us no matter how the self/other boundary gets played out?

Defining Adam as a murderer presupposes that his *core* is that of a murderer. For someone to "be" a murderer he would have to be engaging in killing activities around the clock. I'm "killing" him in my mind by reducing his entire humanity to something he has done once and might have come close to doing on a couple of other occasions. To acknowledge that

259

he is a human being who has killed—who has violent tendencies—opens up the possibility for seeing more in him *and* me.

When I stop pretending that the violence, manipulativeness, and the tendency to exploit isn't exclusively in him, but also in me, then I can see more of our humanity—the sameness inherent in the differences between us.

THE PSYCOPATHIC MONSTER OF A GRANDFATHER

Anne came to see me to help her resolve some conflicts she had with her husband. He wanted to have a child and she did too. An educated woman in her thirties, she was a strong believer in personality being more about genetics than anything else. Anne described her grandfather as a monster and a psychopath. He had raped, molested, used violence and manipulated other people as a way of life. Her own father was no angel either, and she was scared to death of giving birth to a psychopathic monster.

You may be interested to know that Anne defined herself largely by the qualities associated with the other end of the spectrum.

She was an excellent hypnotic subject, and during hypnosis I invited her to imagine the monster in front of her. I invited her to first project all the monster qualities onto him. She told him that he was violent.

For each quality she projected onto him, I invited her to "apply to self". As soon as she reluctantly owned "I am violent" she spontaneously went back to a memory where she had slapped and spit at her husband...then she was invited to view her grandfather through the filter of owning up to her own violence.

She discovered that she could find all the "psychopathic monster" qualities internally and in her own words later said "my grandfather was me". She even found in her grandfather some of her most cherished qualities that had been exclusively hers in that relationship. One example was when during the hypnosis she remembered him once risking his own life to save a child from drowning.

This intervention had a huge effect on Anne. She reported releasing tremendous amounts of fear and anger, and it revitalized her relationship. She reported being more or less ecstatic for a month. She also reported that she had been able to see that she had displayed all the qualities she projected onto her grandfather in the relationship with her husband.

I'm not going to go "all Byron Katie" on you and say that the violent grandfather is exclusively a projection of Anne's mind. Based on his history and what he had done, Anne's views were probably rather accurate and based on detection as well as projection. And that's the point; conflict "out there" is not *exclusively* "out there". It's also a chance to alter your own selfing and discover more of your own complexity. You will be less likely as a result to use others in maintaining a fixed identity.

I imagine that this might be something agents of change with some access to a self-transforming mind might have in common. I suspect that they will be less likely to project onto their client the labels "helpless", "fragile" and "incompetent" in the service of maintaining their identities as all-knowing, wise and smart. The therapist who can find the client inside himself, and who can find qualities associated with therapist inside the client, will have other options available to him.

That doesn't mean you can't accurately detect a sense of vulnerability in your client. It means that you are less likely to project that *role* onto him in the service of maintaining your own identity as strong.

It doesn't mean that you have to have anything to do with

"psychopathic monsters". It doesn't mean that you should pretend that a guy like Adam isn't violent and dangerous. It's just that you acknowledge the dangers and violence in confusing that with all that he is and none of what you are.

I suspect that Anne was somewhere in the socialized/self-authored mid-zone. This way of viewing conflict was alien to her, but very impactful.

I don't know how fair the comparison is between a self-transforming mind and the G-T system or yellow ᵛMEME in Gravesian psychology/Spiral Dynamics. But when I first spoke with Chris Cowan about the capacities of that system, he said that two markers were compulsion dropping off and the relative absence of fear.

At the time I immediately connected this with how quite a few clients whom I have coached in a hybrid REBT way to dispute their musturbating and practice unconditional self-acceptance seem to have those same capacities. Maybe people at earlier stages can gain some of the same capacities by adopting some of the same "habits". When I study Kegan's work and contrast the self-transforming mind with the yellow system in Spiral Dynamics and the late-stage Strategist, Magician and Ironist (the last two stages discovered by Susanne Cook-Greuter), there seems to be some interesting similarities.

Susanne Cook-Greuter has commented that the people at late stages tend to leave conventional organizations, large businesses and institutions. Fear and compulsiveness may reduce naturally as one's meaning-making becomes less absolutistic. There seems to be a common, seemingly paradoxical, movement of the self being deconstructed as an illusion while also being reconstructed as bigger. More and more of the world can be taken as object and identified with. We can find more of our common humanity by seeing more of "me" in others and more of others in "me".

This is perhaps a bit one-sided, though. It's important to differentiate between having a capacity and using it. A self-sovereign person might act kindly if you don't challenge, and a self-transforming mind may perhaps use his capacity to become a better and crueler psychopath.

Do realize that there are many other factors besides an individual's meaning-making capacity that determine if and how he may use that capacity. Having power can often contribute to being less likely to take others' perspectives. Being "the underdog" might out of necessity stimulate better perspective-taking.

Unresolved issues can be reactivated and we may regress. Pain, depression and disease can contribute to us becoming more egocentric.

YOUR SELF-TRANSFORMING CAPABILITIES

I'm going to end by offering some ideas around how you can trigger more self-transforming capacities.

- Shadow work: The type of work I did with Anne is great for expanding the self and to loosen rigid dichotomies.

- Meditation on the body sensations of certainty: This practice helps to acknowledge that the sensations of certainty are just that.

- Questioning certainty: Learn to equate the sense of having a *complete* understanding with death. It's time to re-engage and ask what you are missing.

- Cultivate great bartenders and receptionists.

Other people will see your blind spots better than you do. Seek out feedback from a variety of sources, *especially* from people operating out of different frameworks so that feedback isn't just used to strengthen your current stance or agenda, but so that it may alert you to flaws and blind spots as well.

Happy hunting!
Jørgen